Fashion Illustration
TECHNIQUES FOR BEGINNERS
By Anna Nadler

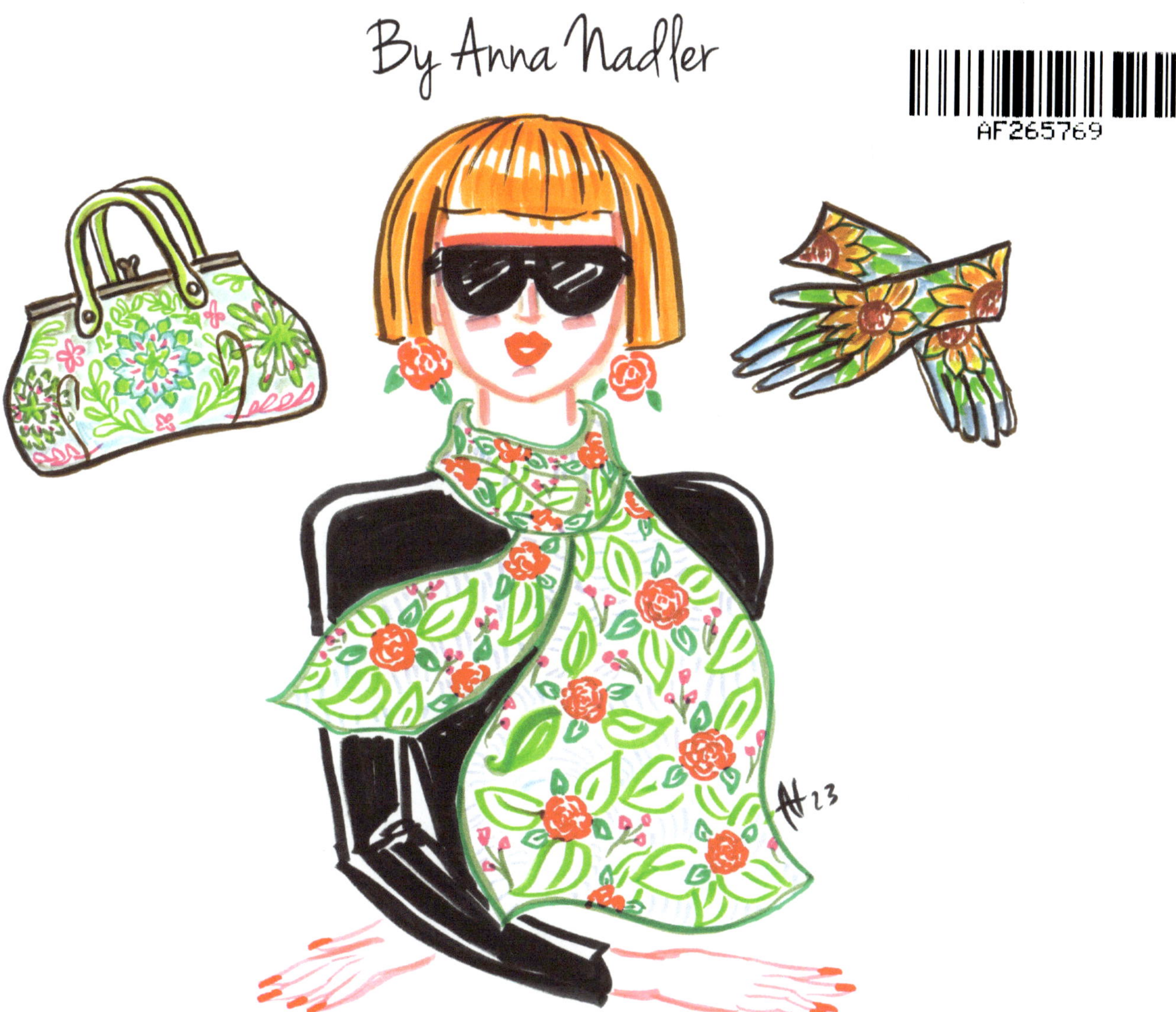

Copyright © 2023 Anna Nadler
All rights reserved
Published by Anna Nadler Art
No part of this publication may be
reproduced, stored in a retrieval system or
transmitted in any form or by any means,
electronic, mechanical, photocopying, recording
or otherwise, without prior written permission
from the author/publisher.
www.annanadlerart.com

ISBN: 9781958428313

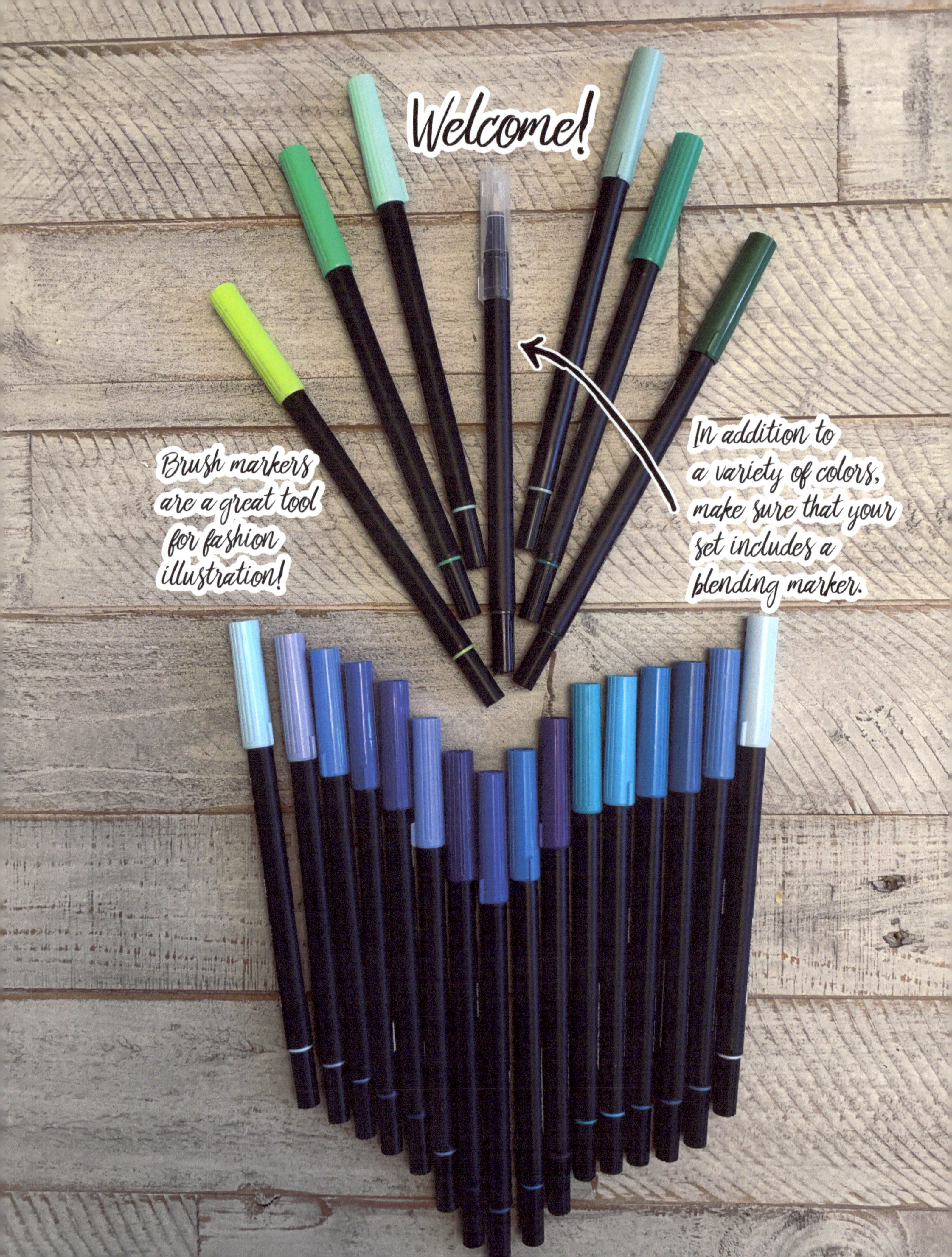

Welcome!
Brush markers are a great tool for fashion illustration!
In addition to a variety of colors, make sure that your set includes a blending marker.

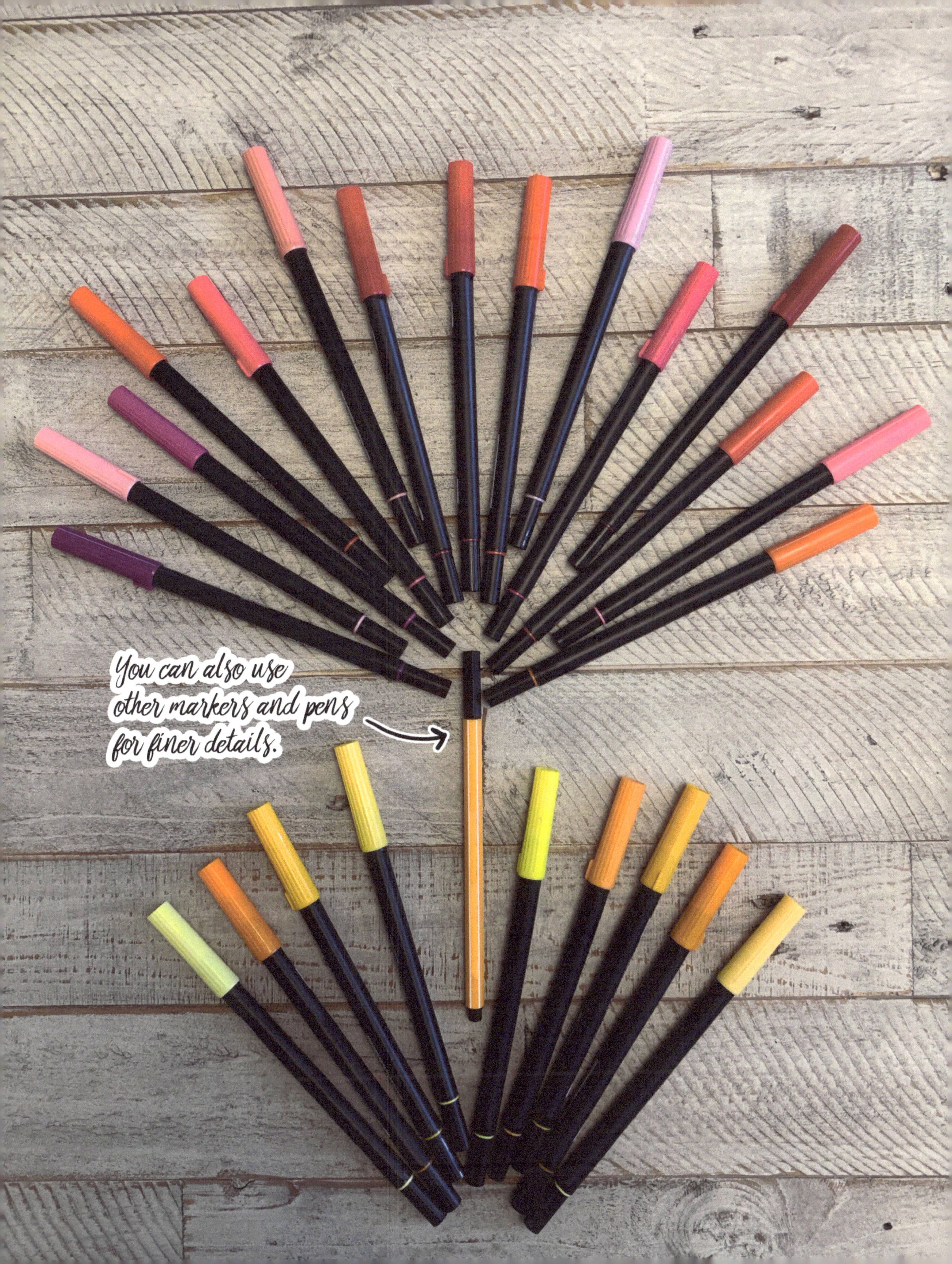
You can also use other markers and pens for finer details.

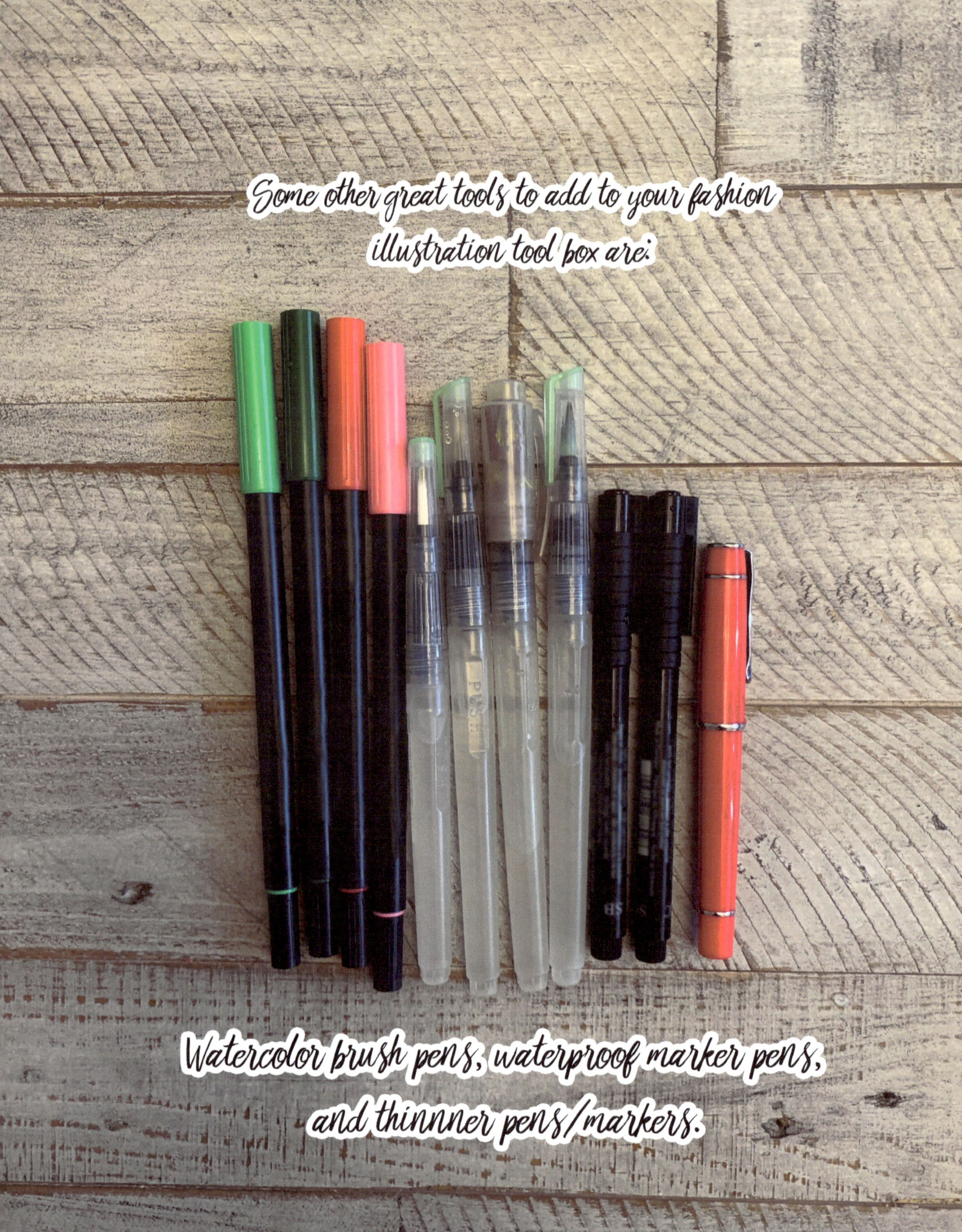
Some other great tools to add to your fashion illustration tool box are:
Watercolor brush pens, waterproof marker pens, and thinnner pens/markers.

Now, let's get started drawing fashion!

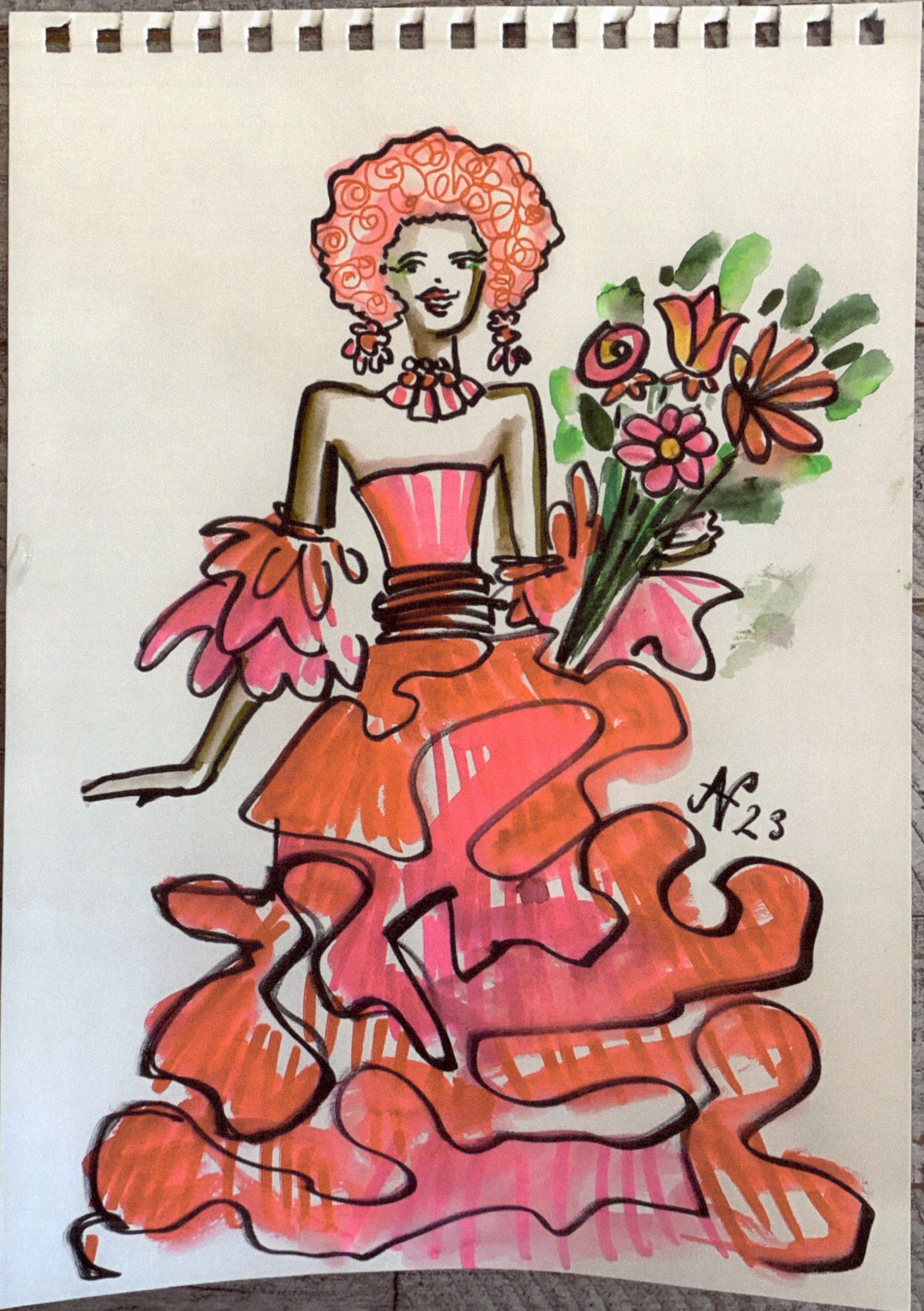

Fashion Figures

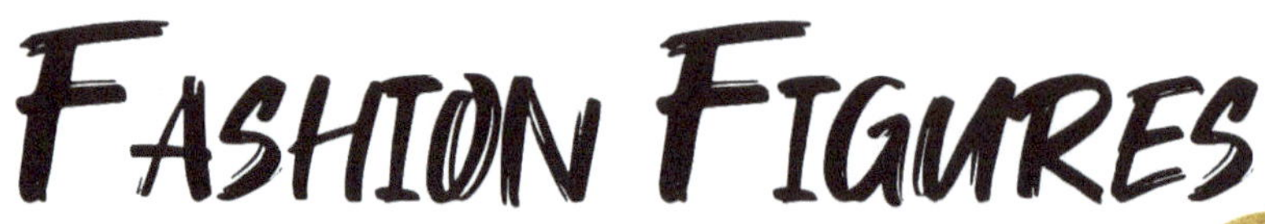

Fashion figures are drawn in a way to show the beauty of the clothes.

Poses can be dynamic or simple.

Start with a line drawing. Then color in your figures.

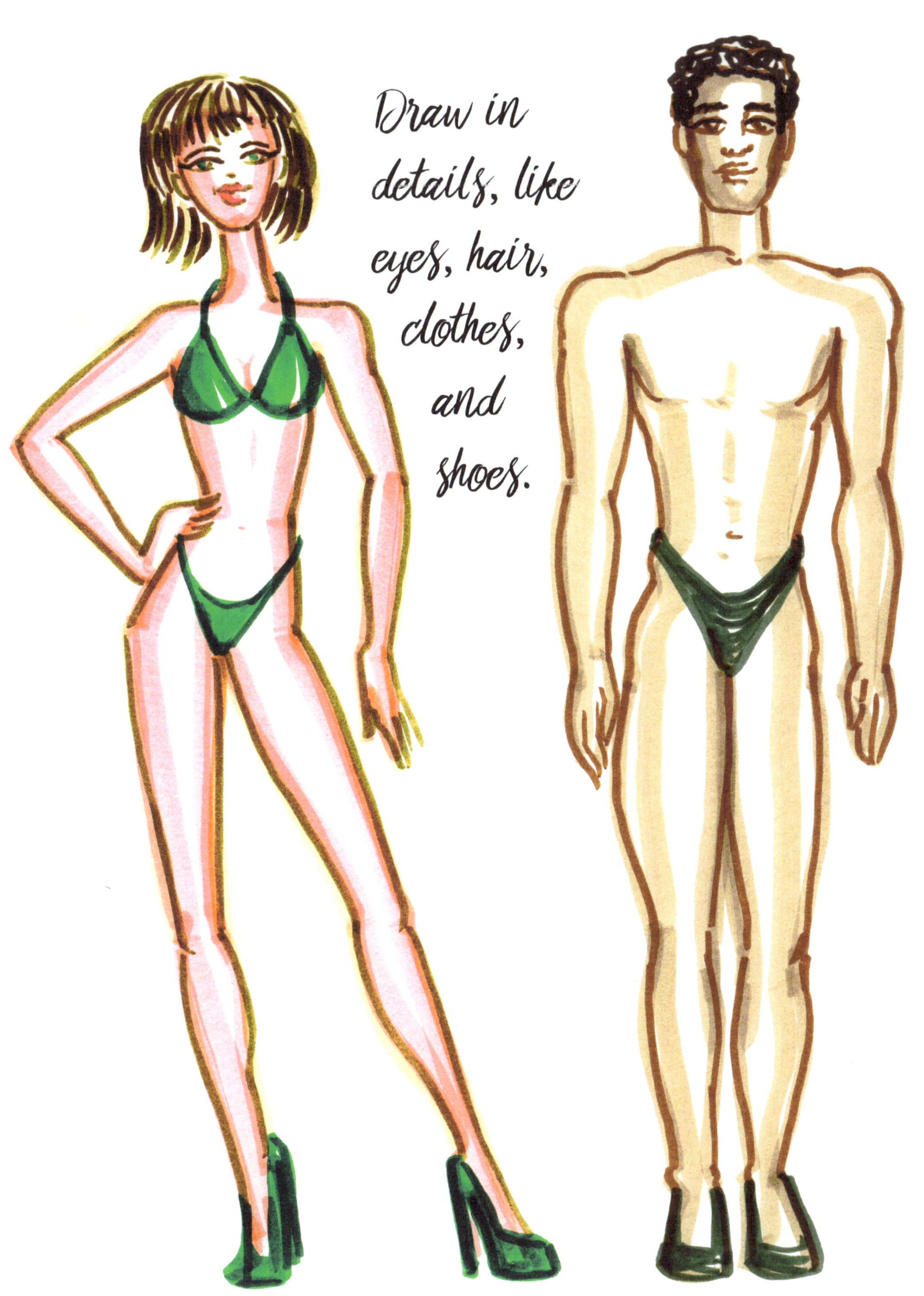

Draw in
details, like
eyes, hair,
clothes,
and
shoes.

DRAWING FACES

Start with a line drawing, then choose a skin tone. You can experiment with leaving more or less highlight on the faces and hair. Try to draw loosely, with strong, decisive lines. Do not go over the same place too many times with the marker, this tends to destroy paper and make your art look labored.

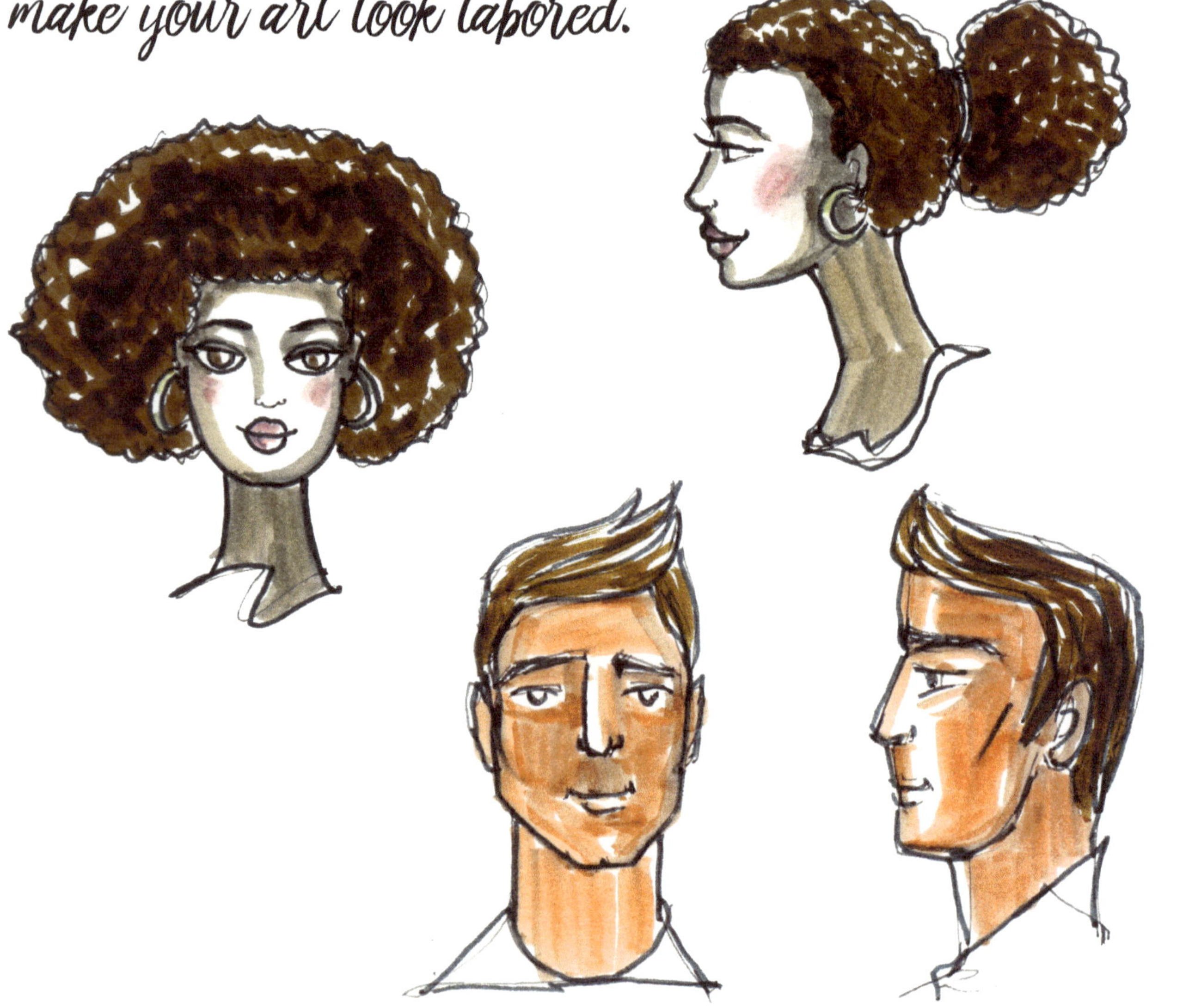

Pay attention to different features, hair textures, skin tones. Do not draw the same mannequin face for everyone. We are all unique. Tastefully emphasize each person's attributes.

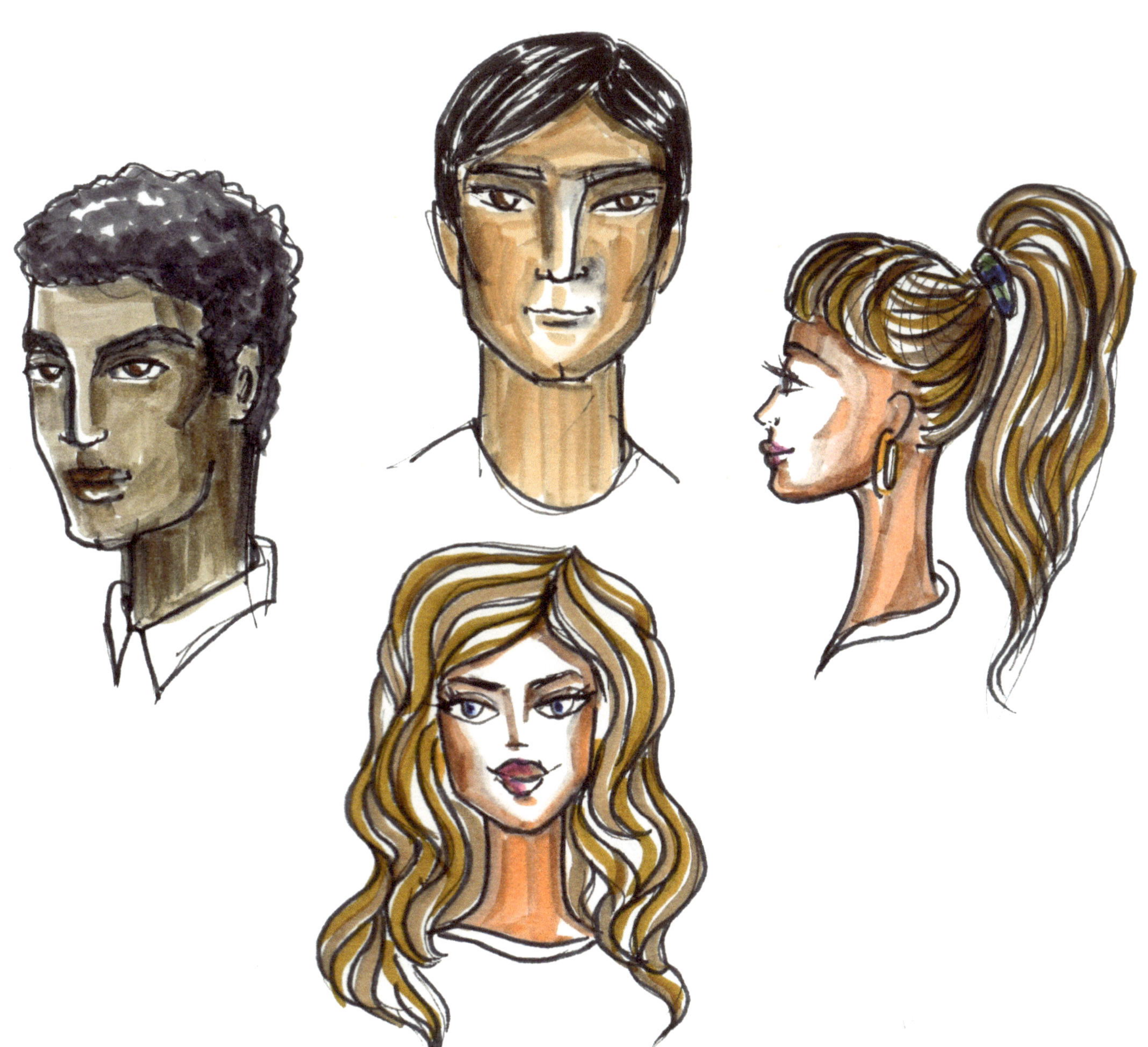

Female Hands

Women usually have small, delicate hands.
The gestures are feminine and expressive.

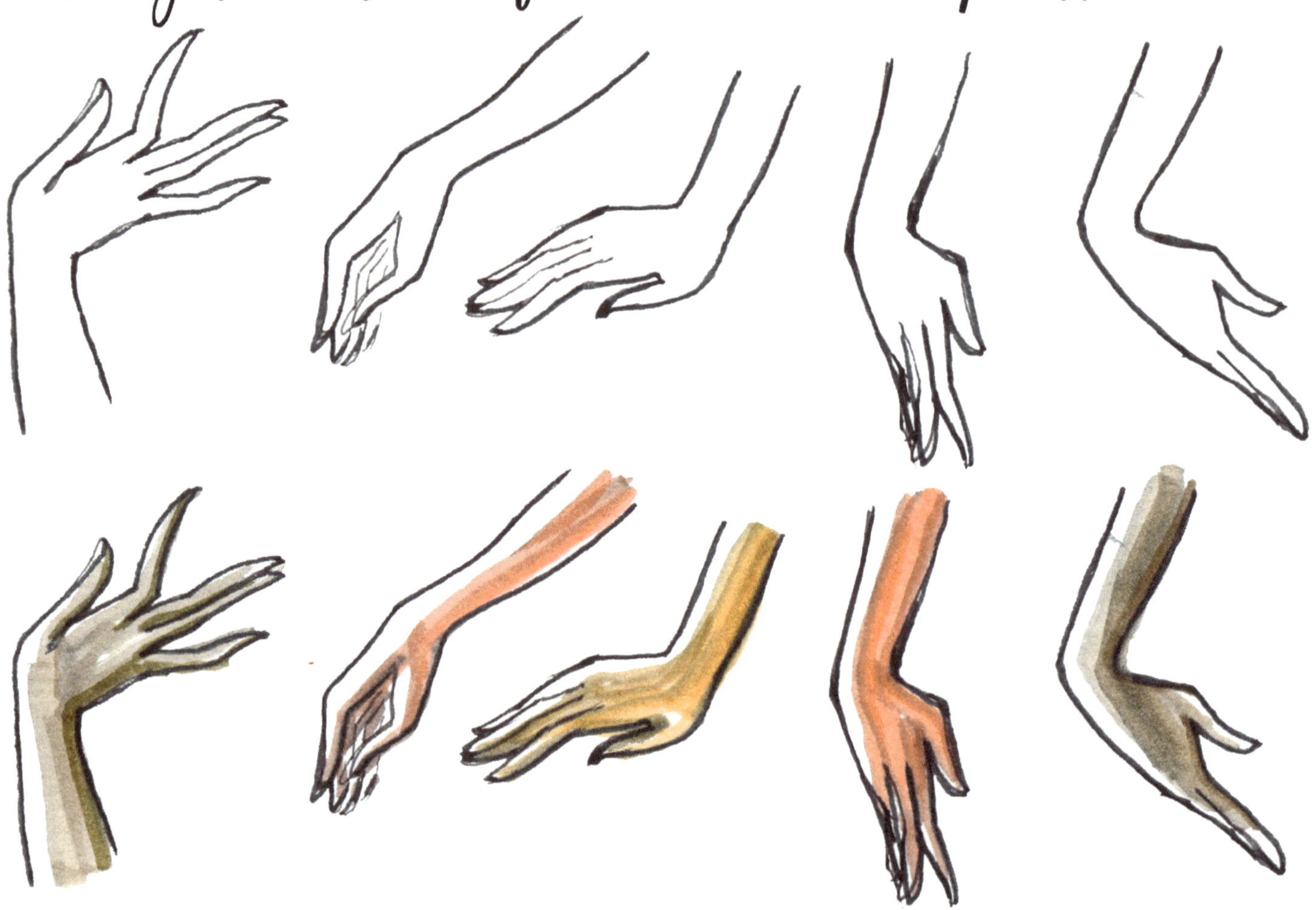

Experiment with various skin tone colors.
To add shade, add outline in the same color.
For highlights, leave a side where the light
hits — the paper color or white.

Male Hands

Men have larger and wider hands than women. They are muscular with less expression and a boxy shape.

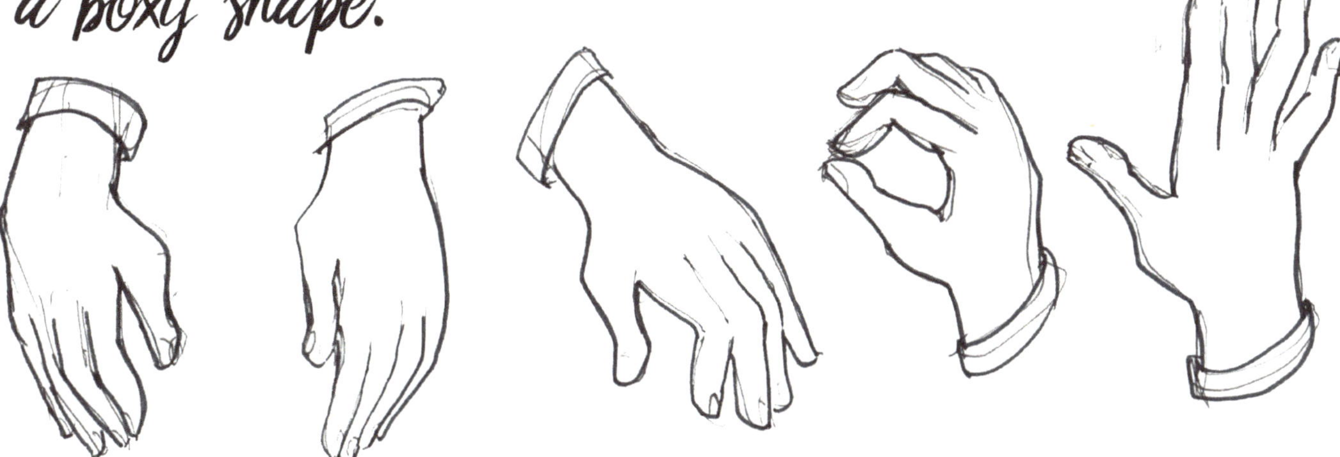

Experiment with various skin tone colors. To add shade, add outline in the same color.

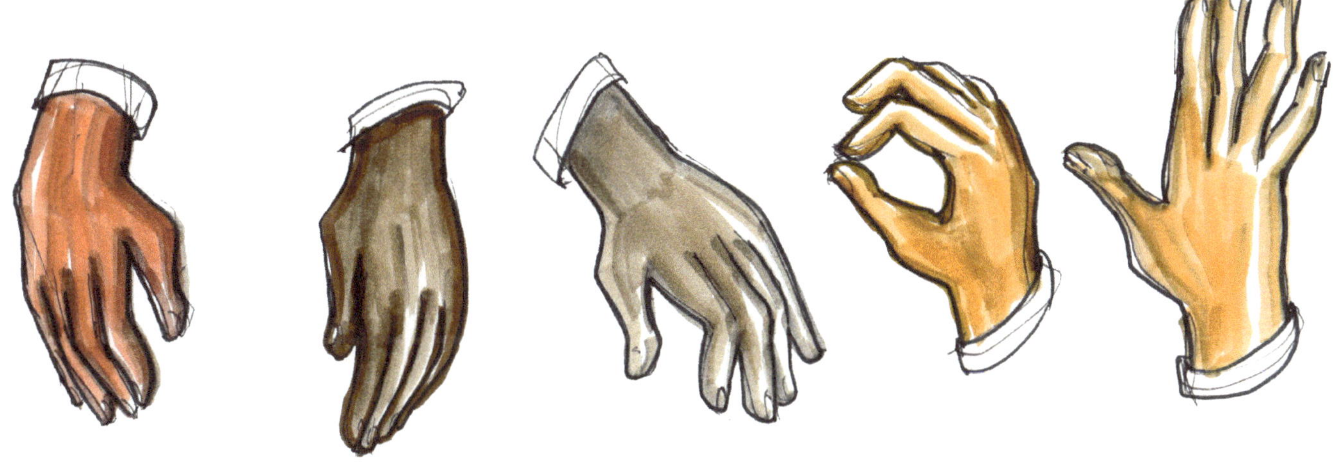

Profile Views

Sometimes we can draw our people in a profile view. As always, keep it simple. Indicate the lips, lashes, ears, cheeks with simple lines. Do not over-render. You can add slightly more detail for closeups.

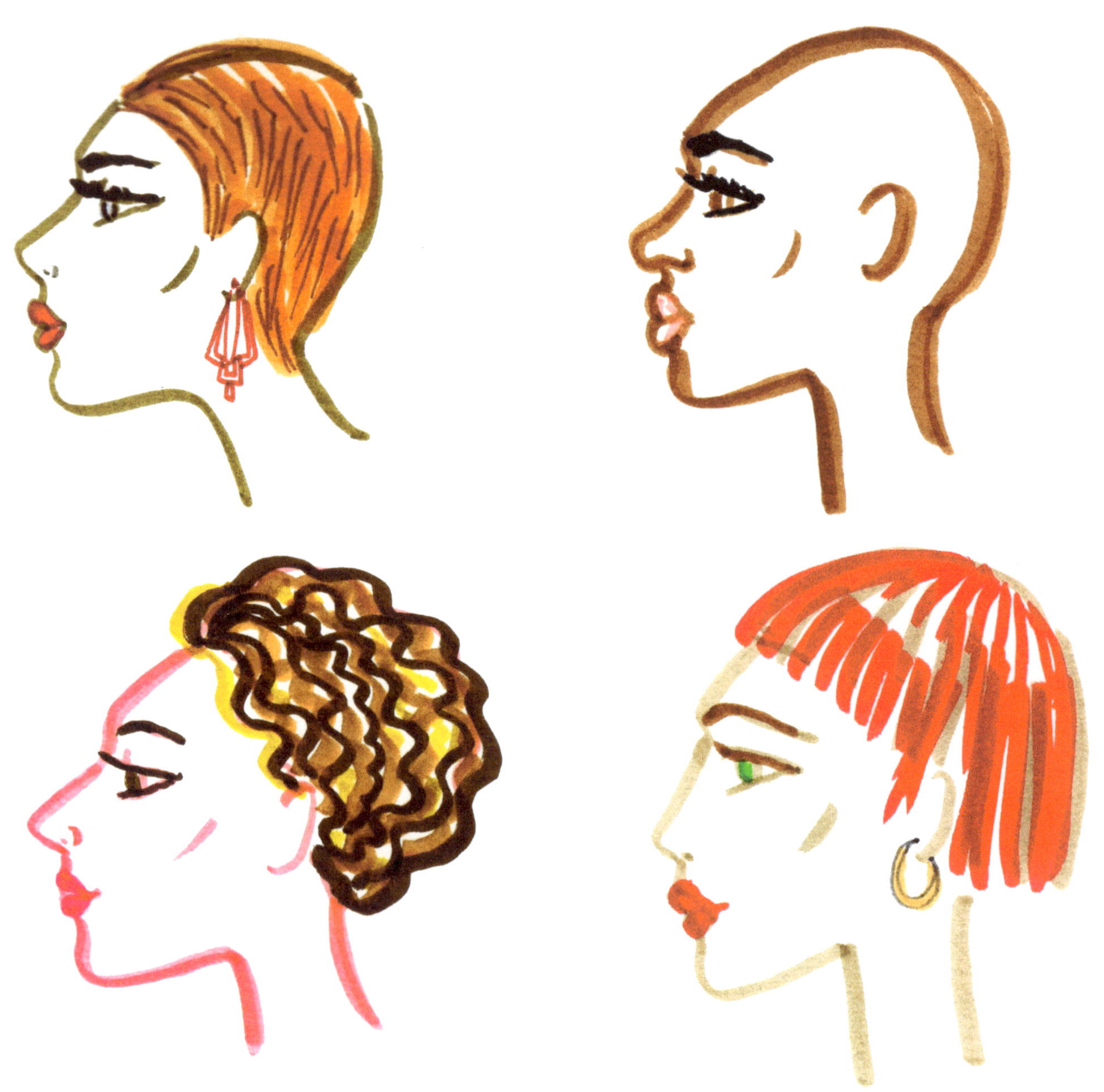

Facial Features

When we do portraits or closeups of our fashion figures, or when we wish to showcase earrings, hats, necklaces, etc, we want to add extra detail to the rendering of the persons' faces. Play with blending techniques and shading, as well as colors. You can make a statement with simple lines for a nose, lips or lashes.

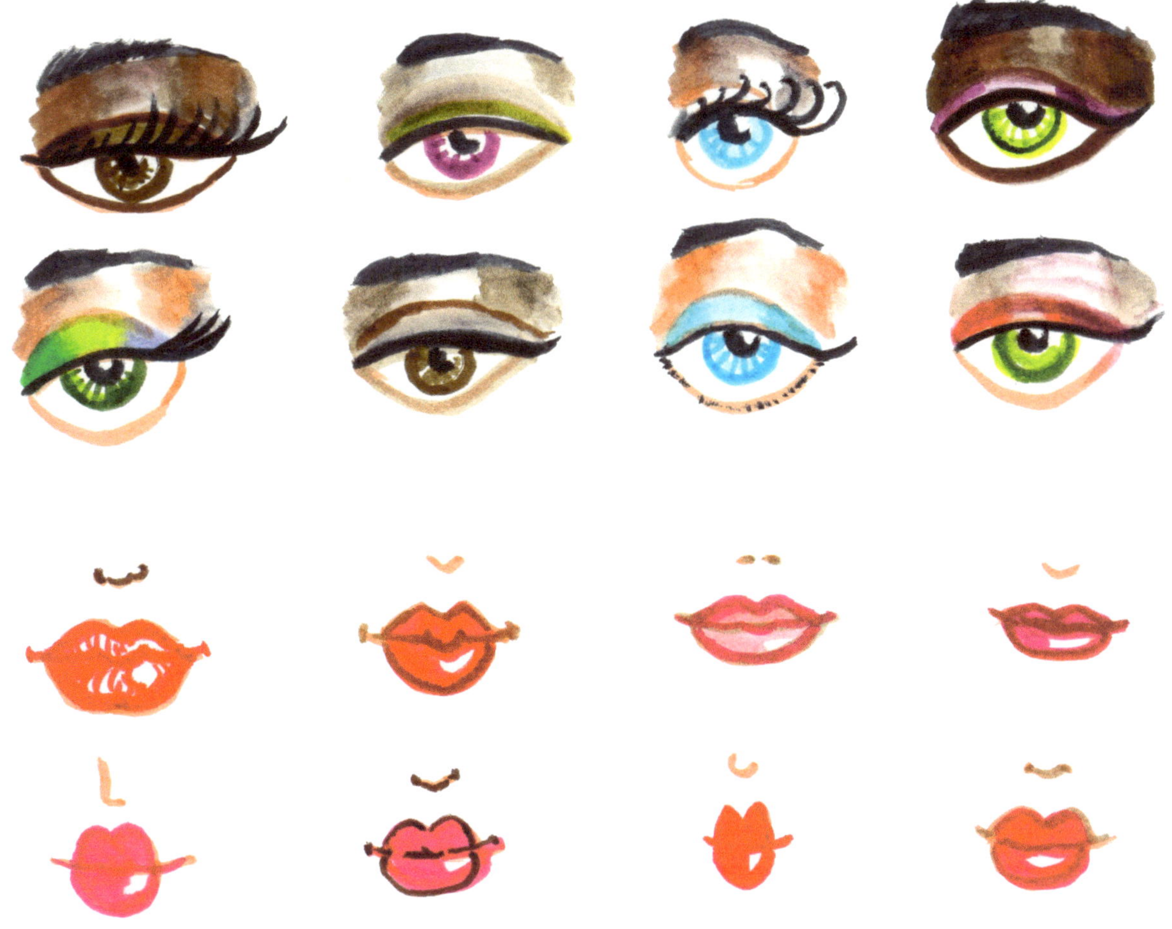

Color Blends

You can create
a variety of
beautiful color
combinations
by juxtaposing
similar and
contrasting
colors. Blend
lighter colors
into the darker
ones. You may
also use a
blending marker.

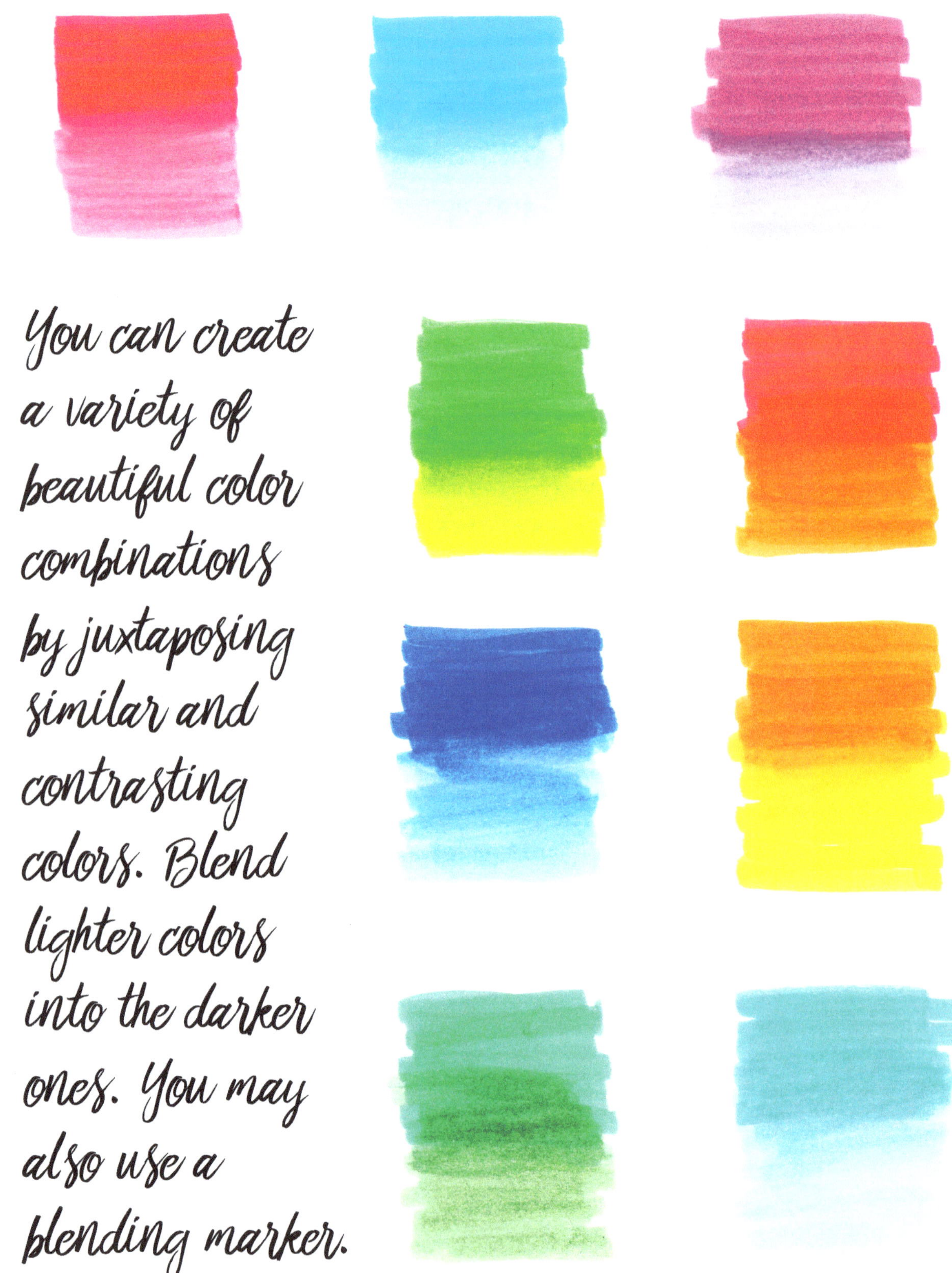

Lines and Markings

Brush markers are great at producing a wide variety of lines and markings. Feel free to experiment making the ones you see here.

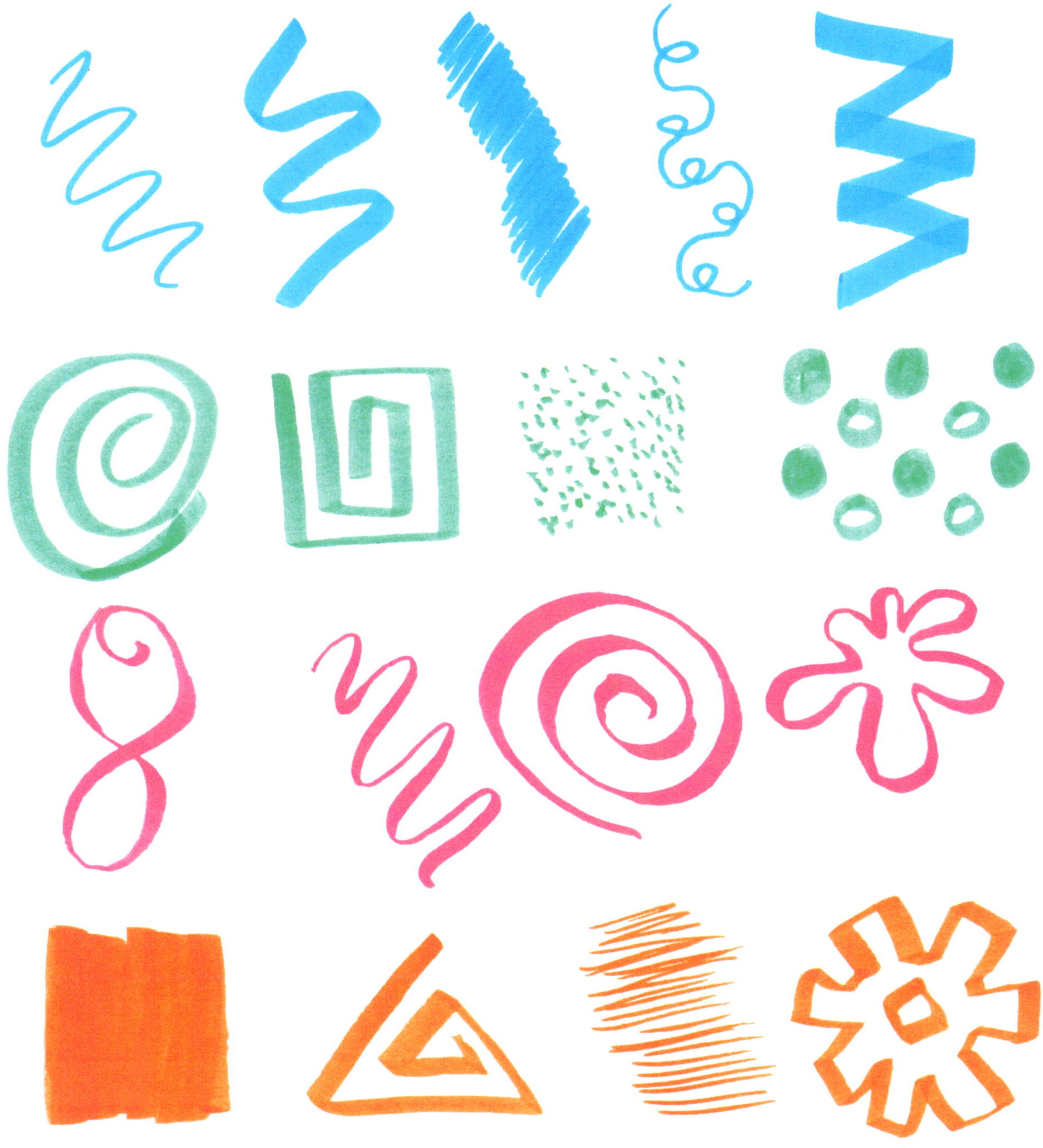

Classic Prints

Pay attention to various prints you see on clothing and accessories. There are classic prints and more novelty/fun prints.

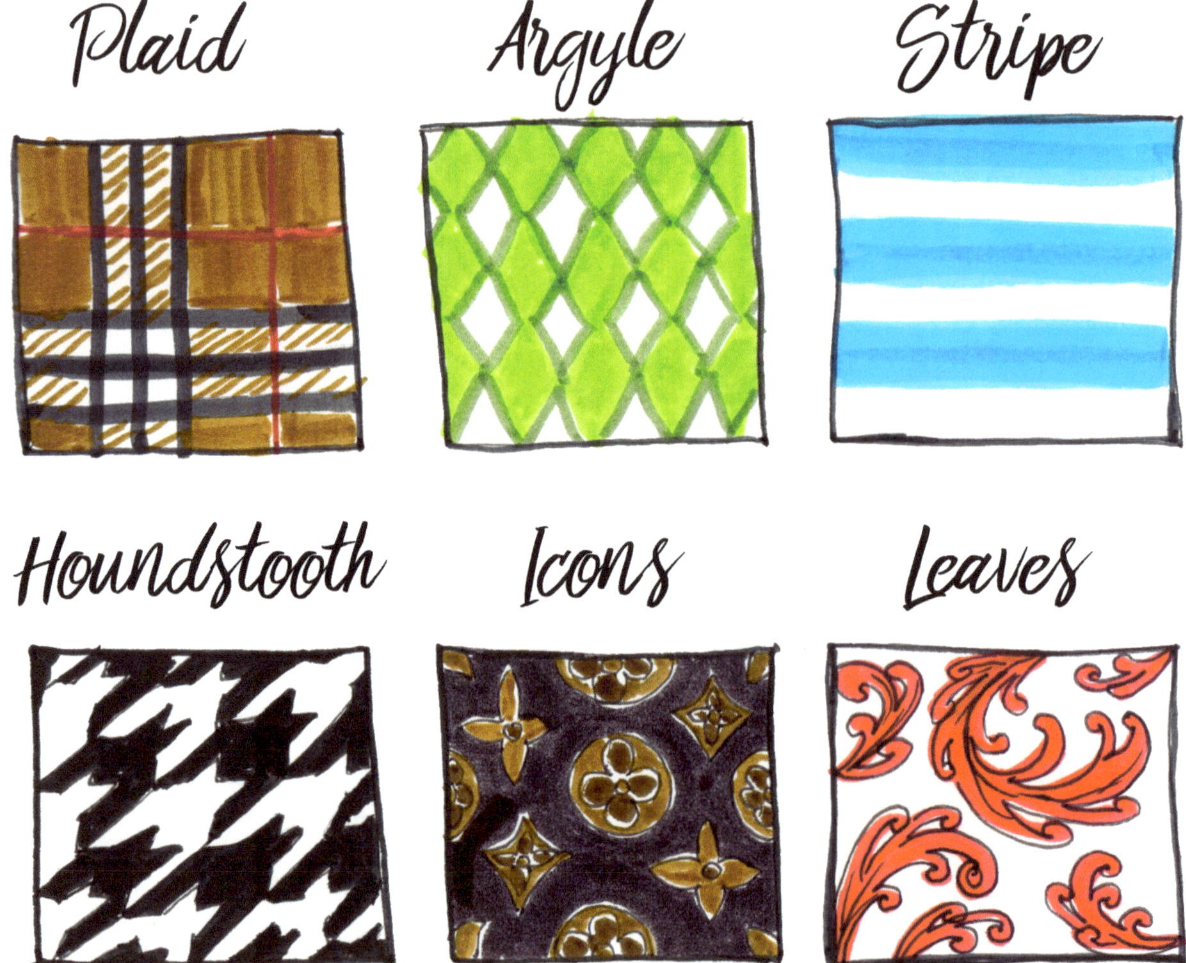

Here are some examples of classic prints. There are also monogram, paisley, polka dots, pin stripes, other variety of argyle prints, and more. See how prints look on folds and different textures.

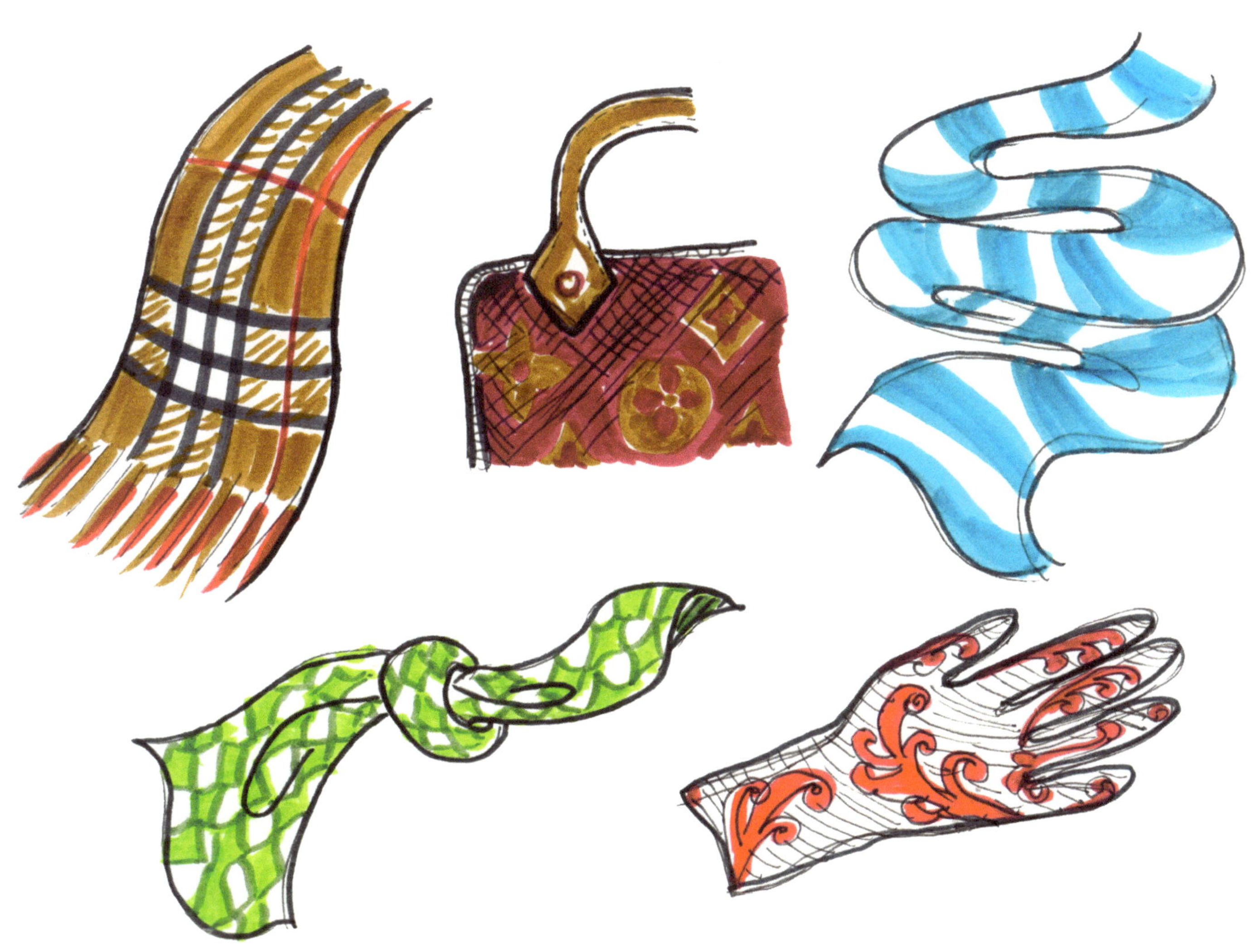

Fun Prints

There are a number of various fun prints and patterns. These include floral, geometric combinations, spirals and swirls, waves, dots of various sizes and more.

Geometric

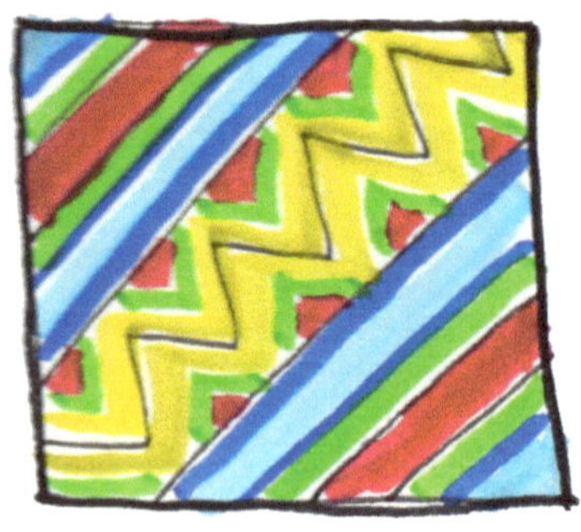

Nature

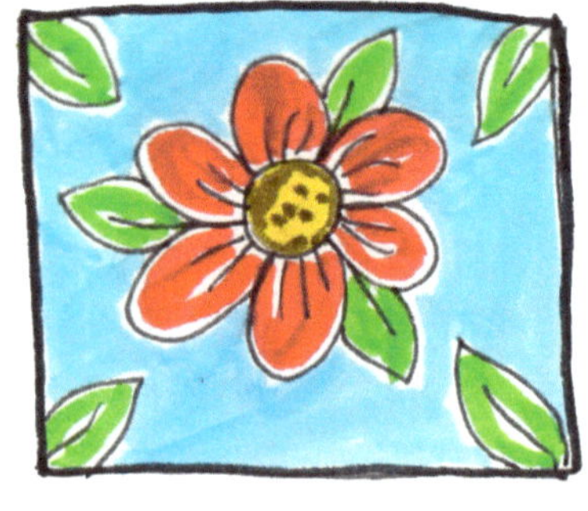

Swirls

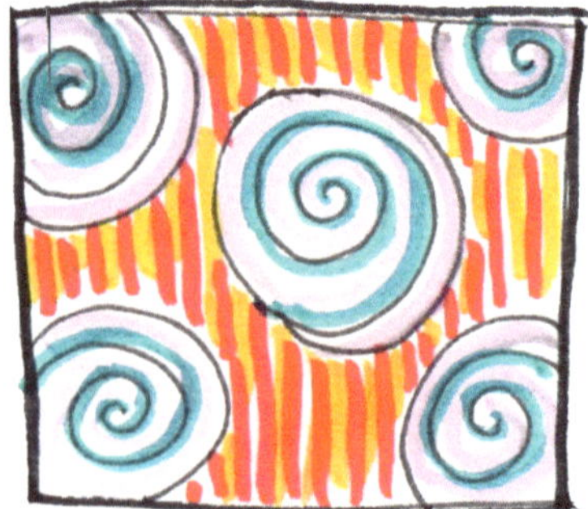

Dots

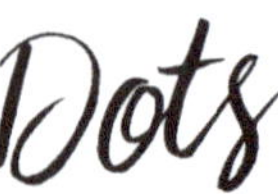

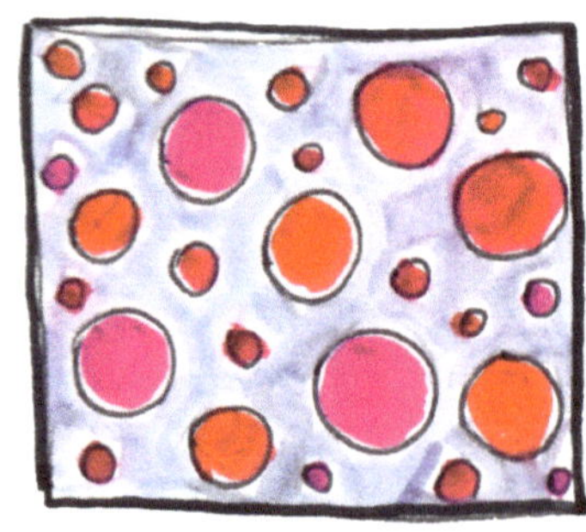

Waves

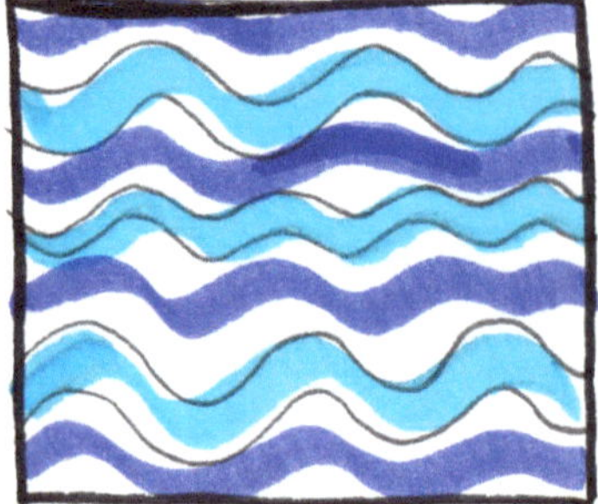

Floral

The next time you see a fun print, pay attention
to the way it drapes when worn on a body, or
when hanging on a chair. We can indicate folds
with simple lines, then shift the print a bit off
to the side, as it continues past the fold.

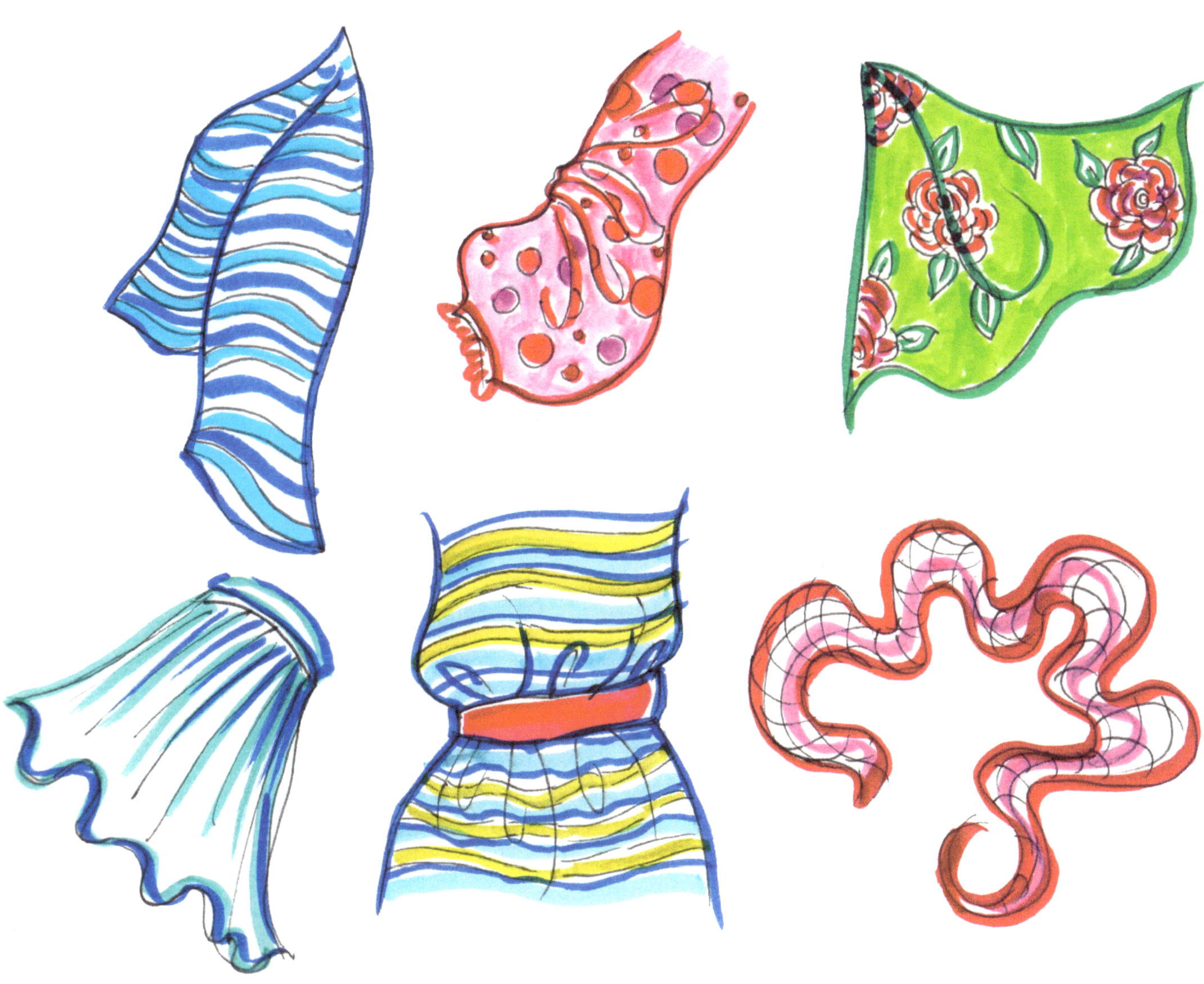

Preppy Style

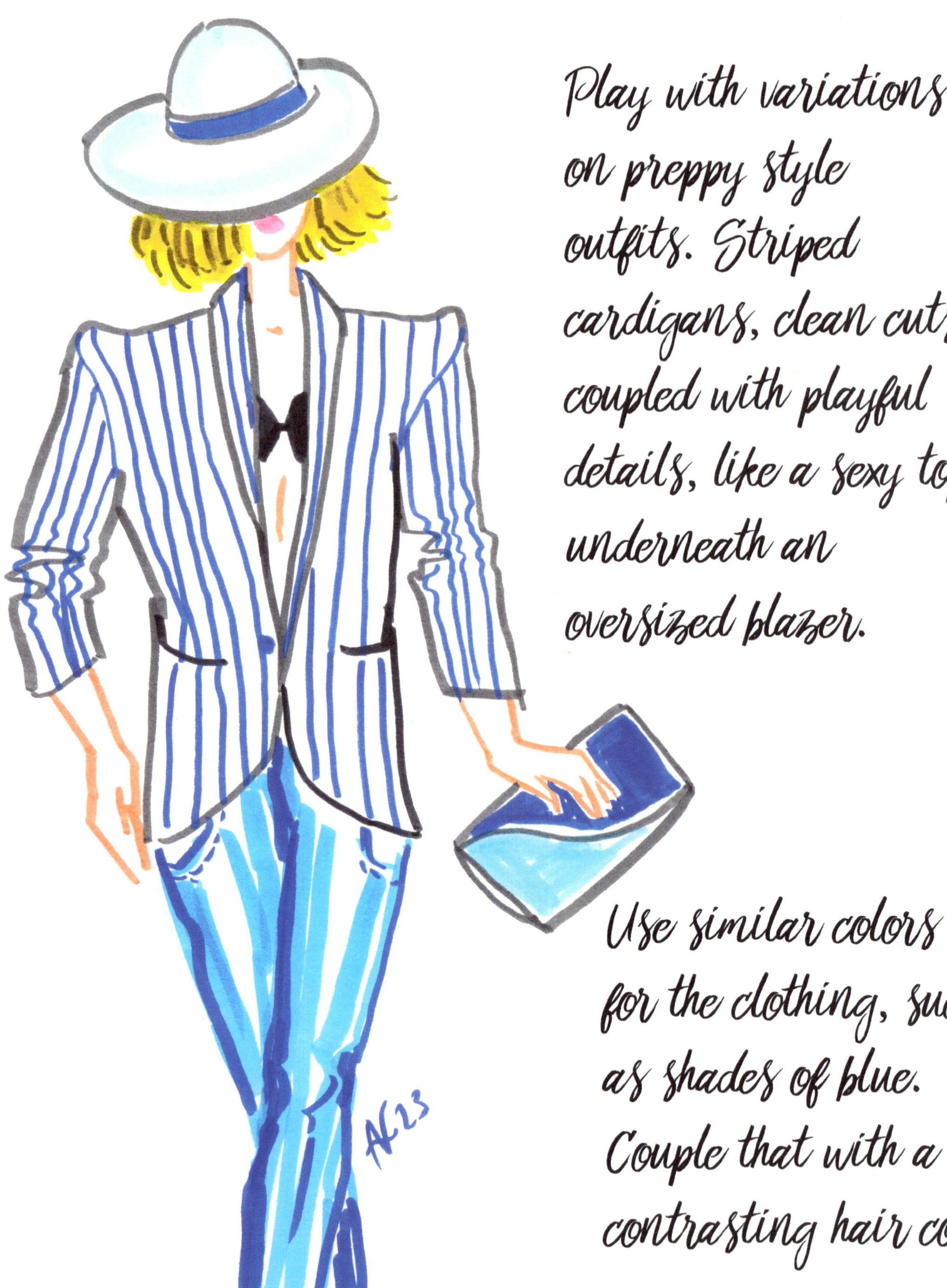

Play with variations on preppy style outfits. Striped cardigans, clean cuts, coupled with playful details, like a sexy top underneath an oversized blazer.

Use similar colors for the clothing, such as shades of blue. Couple that with a contrasting hair color.

Bohemian Style

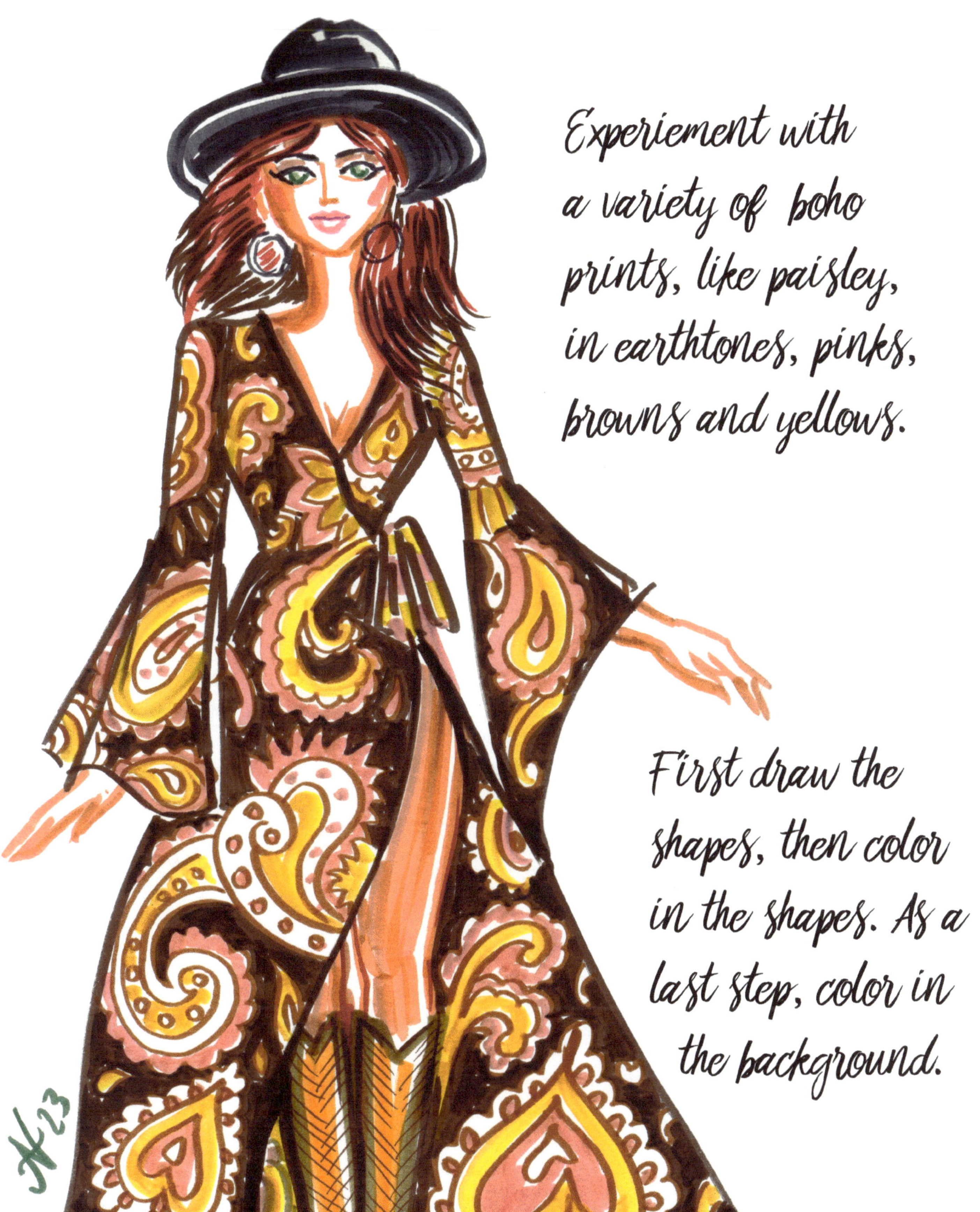

Experiement with
a variety of boho
prints, like paisley,
in earthtones, pinks,
browns and yellows.

First draw the
shapes, then color
in the shapes. As a
last step, color in
the background.

Drawing Eveningwear

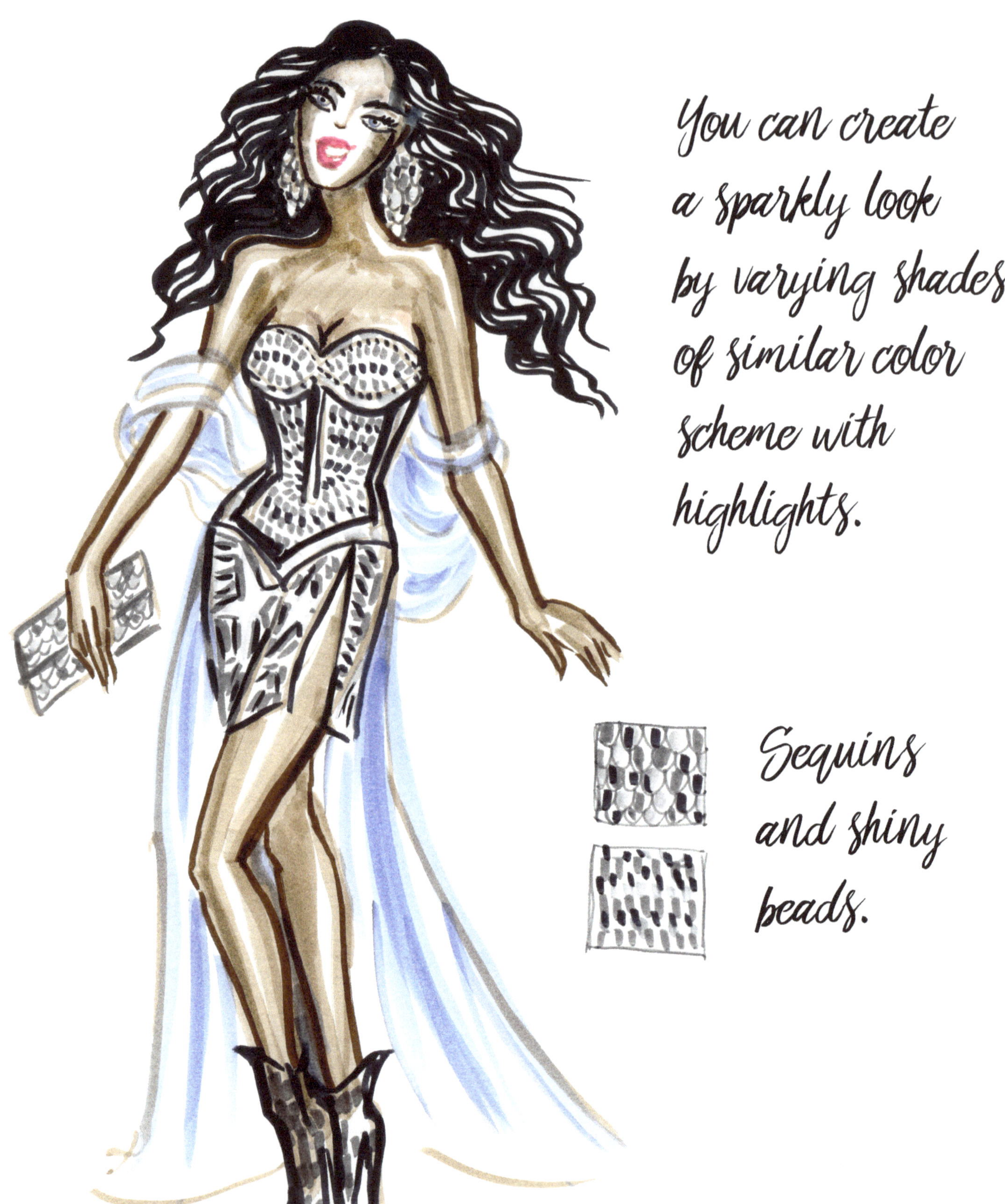

You can create a sparkly look by varying shades of similar color scheme with highlights.

Sequins and shiny beads.

Shiny Textures

Key to making a shiny or sparkly material look is strategically leaving shiny areas white or the color of the paper, if it is light.

Follow these steps to build texture.

1
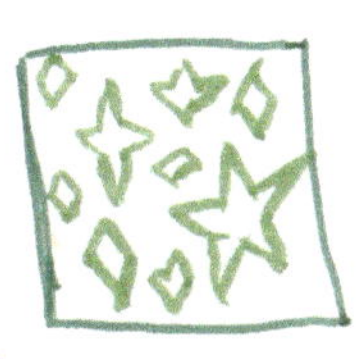

2
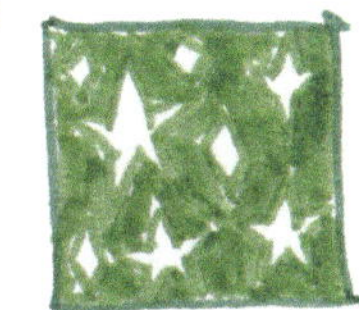

3
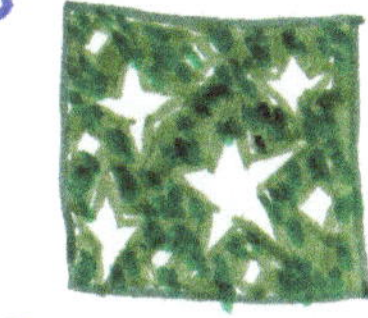

4
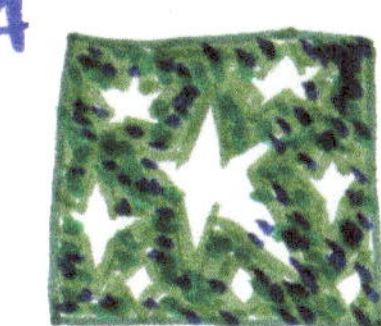

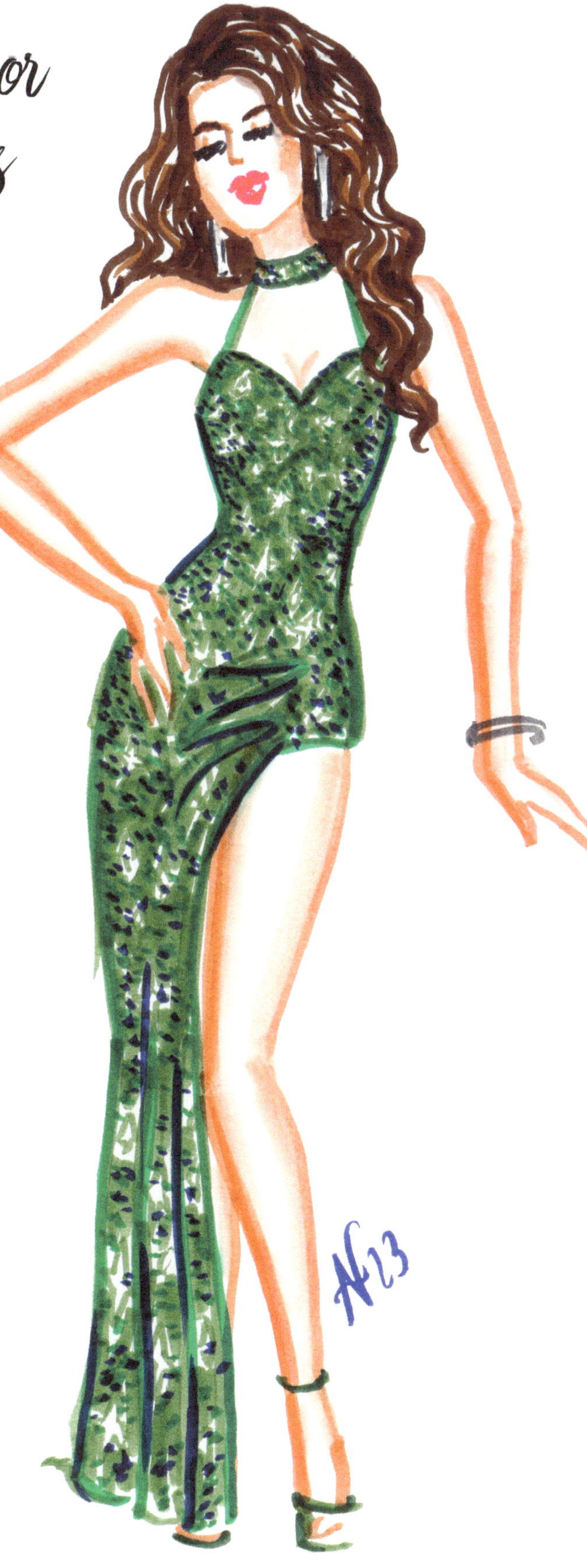

Animal Prints

Drawing animal prints such as leopard, zebra, cheetah and more is fun! Animal prints are always chic and never go out of style. Try creating some of these prints.

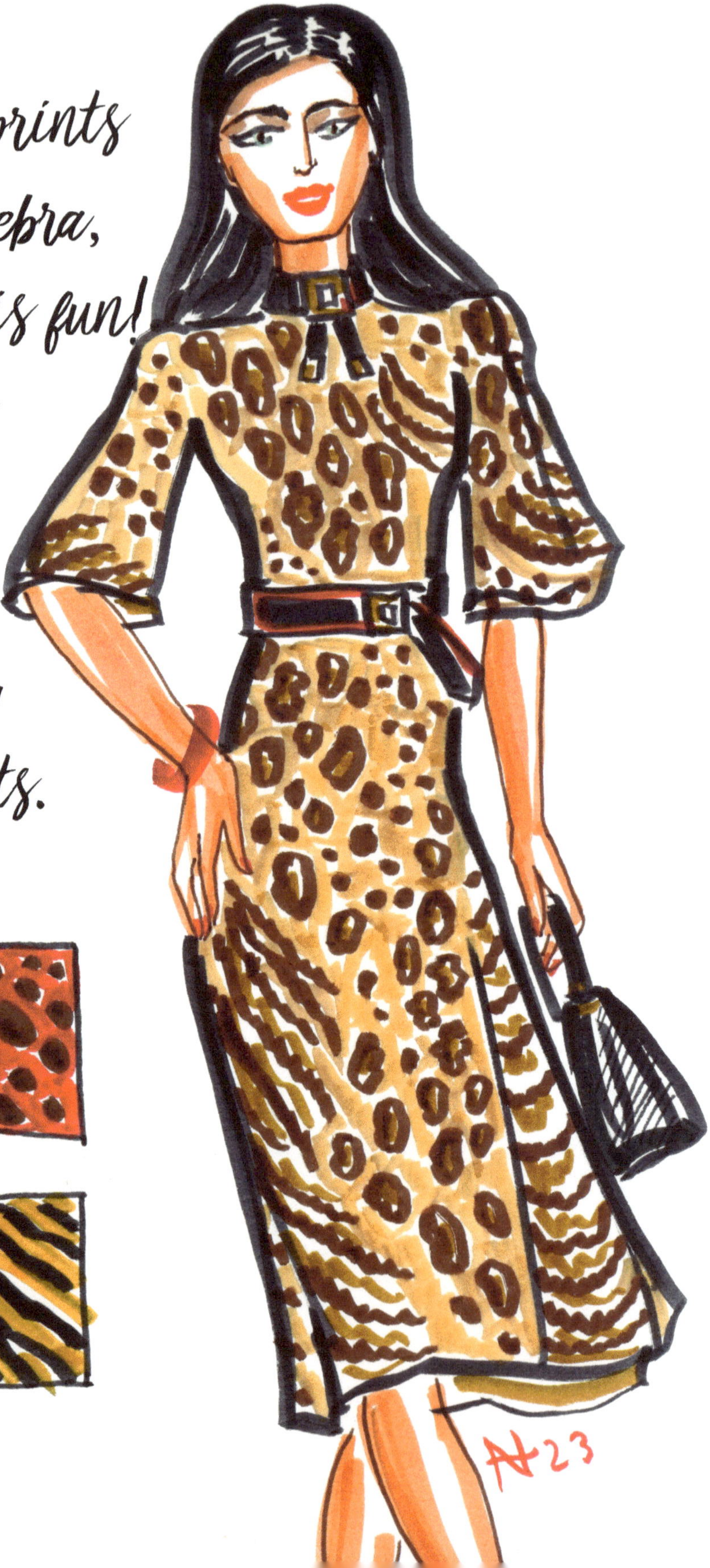

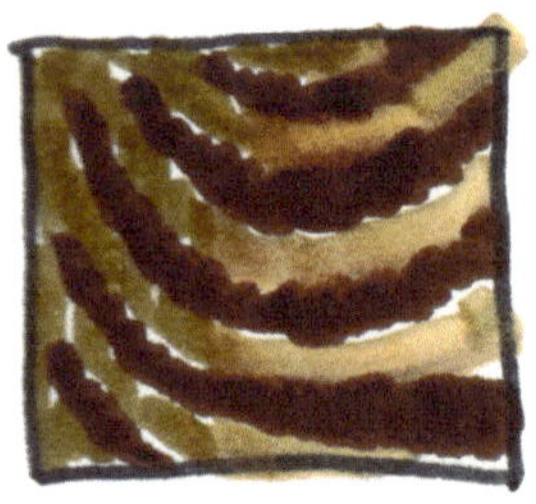
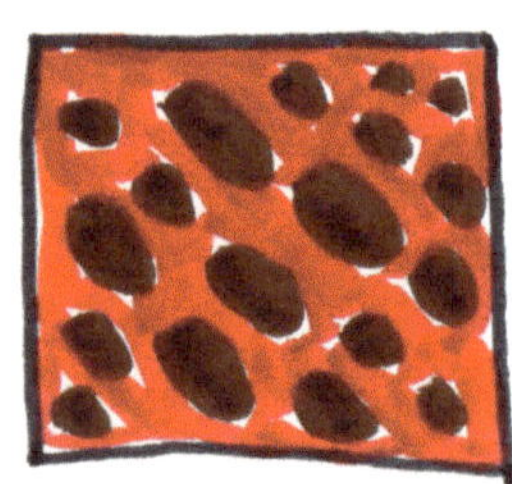
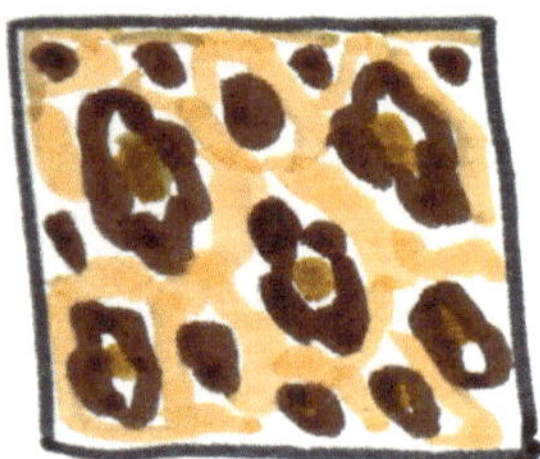
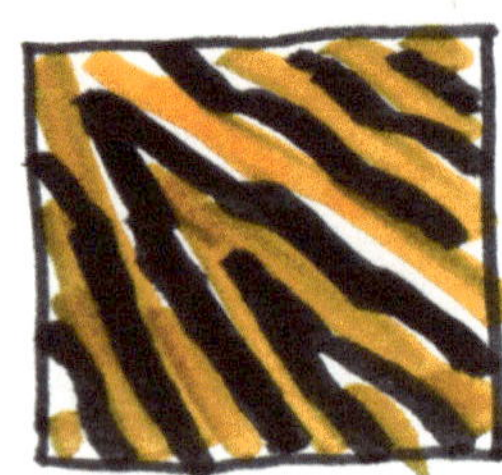

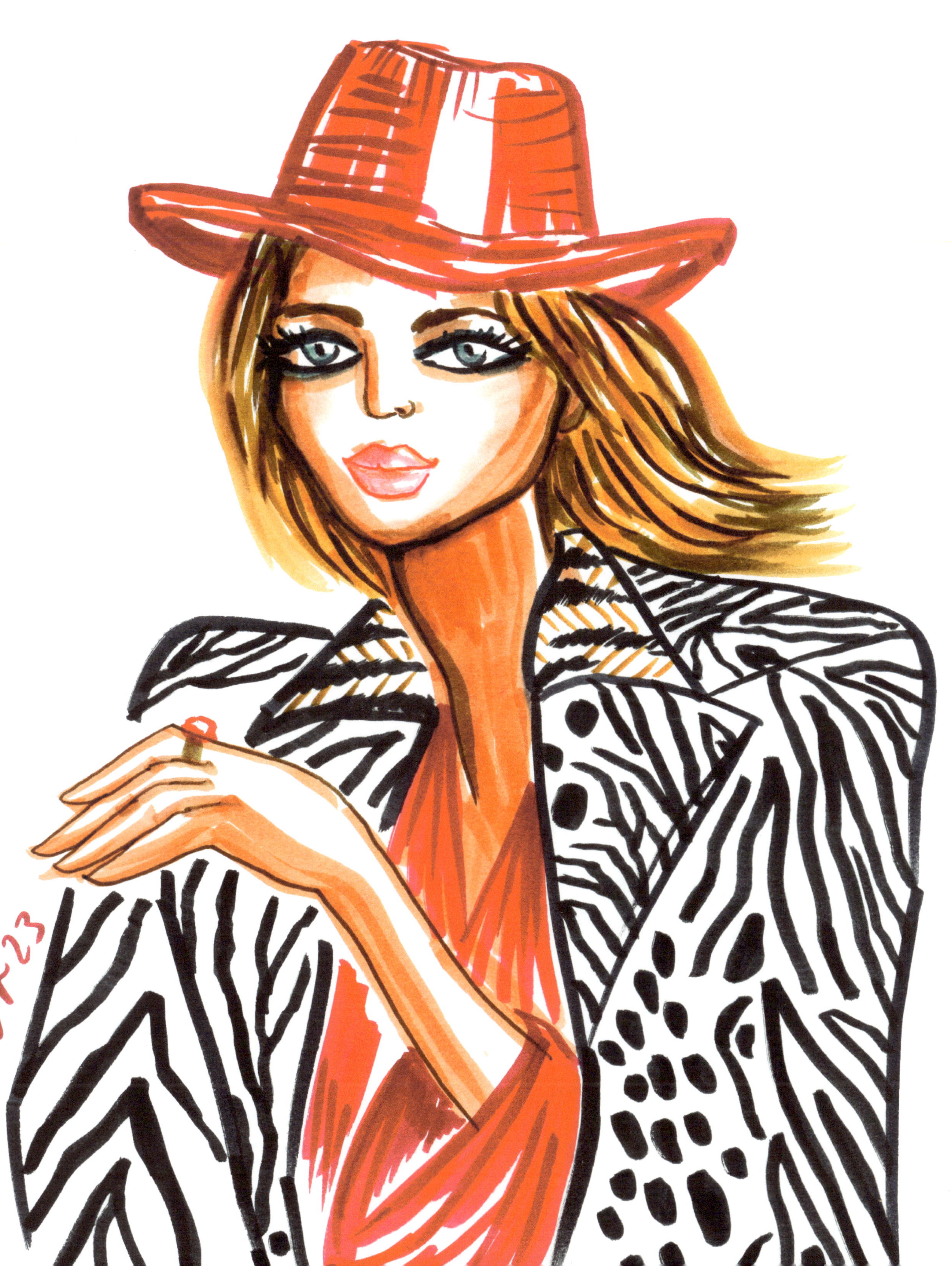

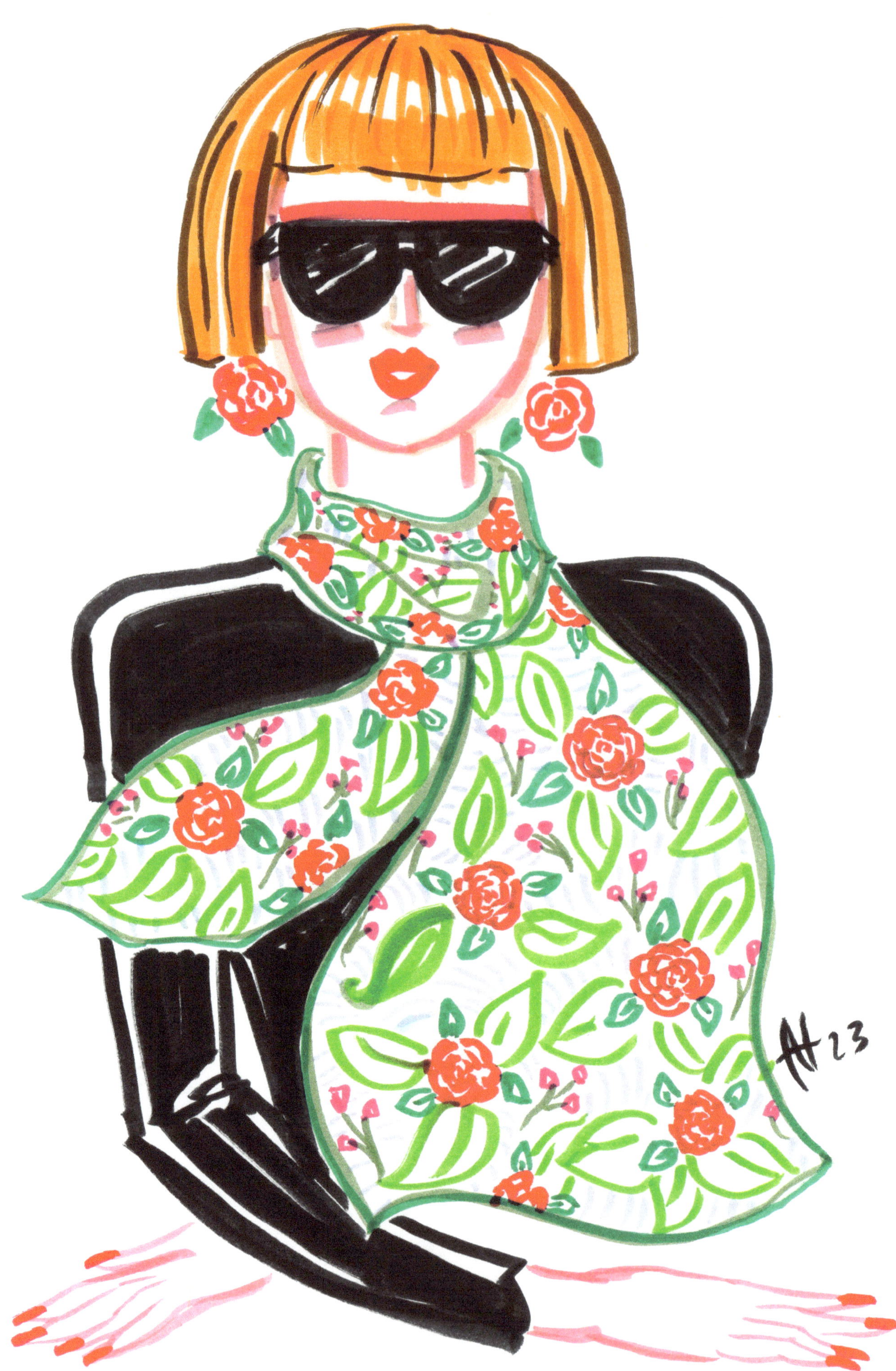

Floral Prints

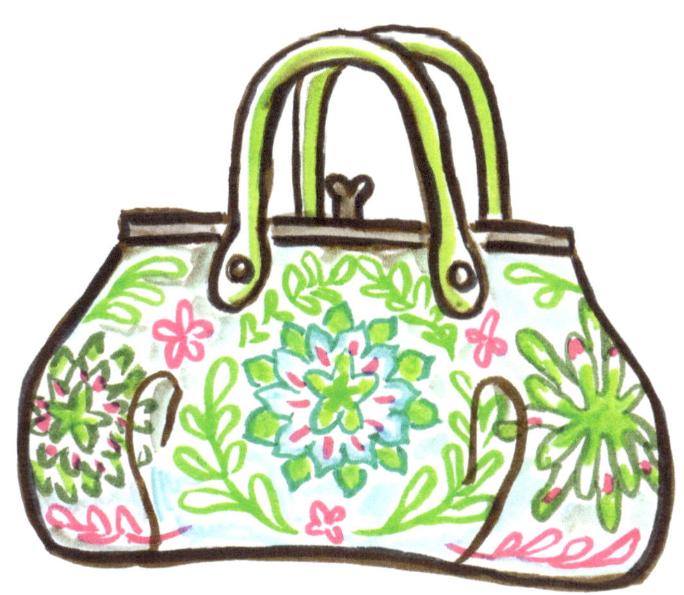

Flowers make a great theme for fashion. They look fabulous on clothing and accessories for all seasons!

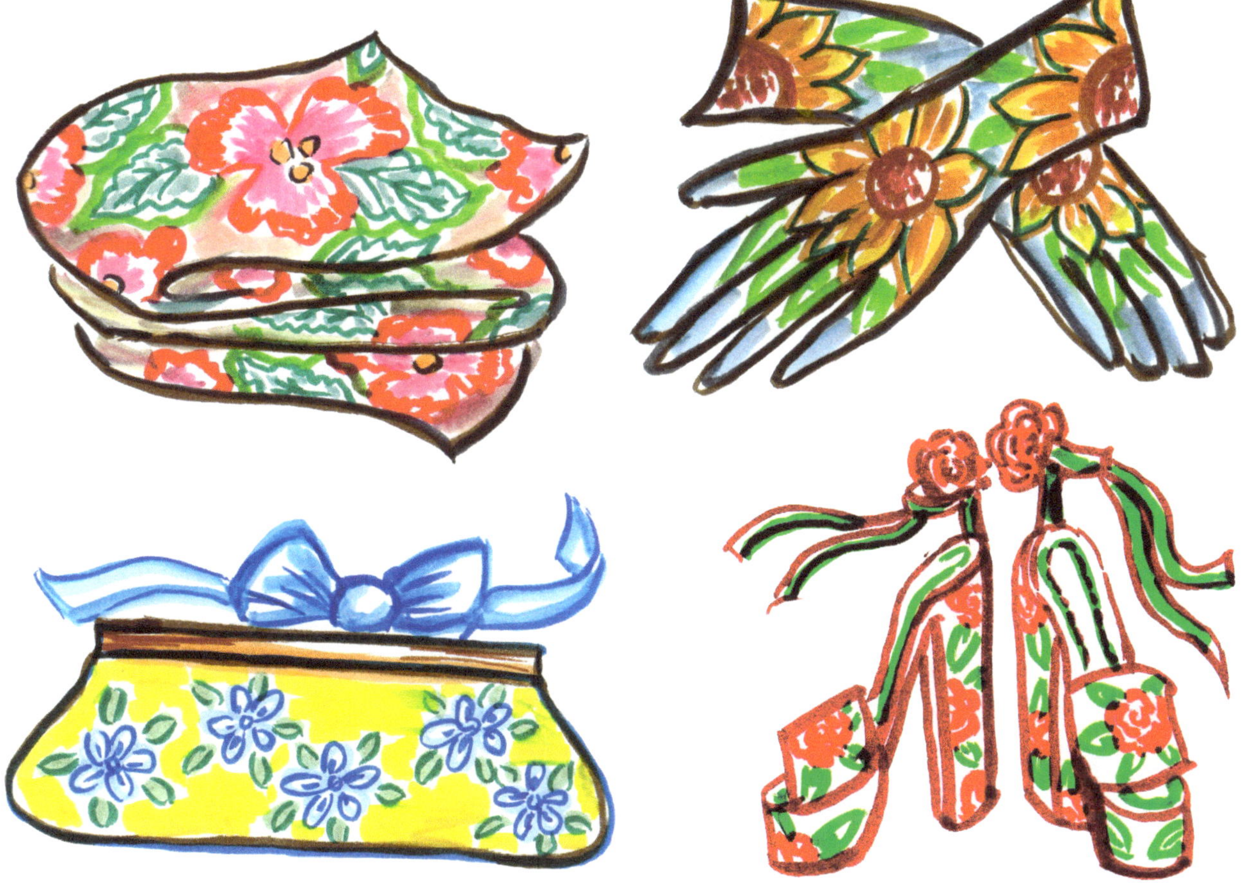

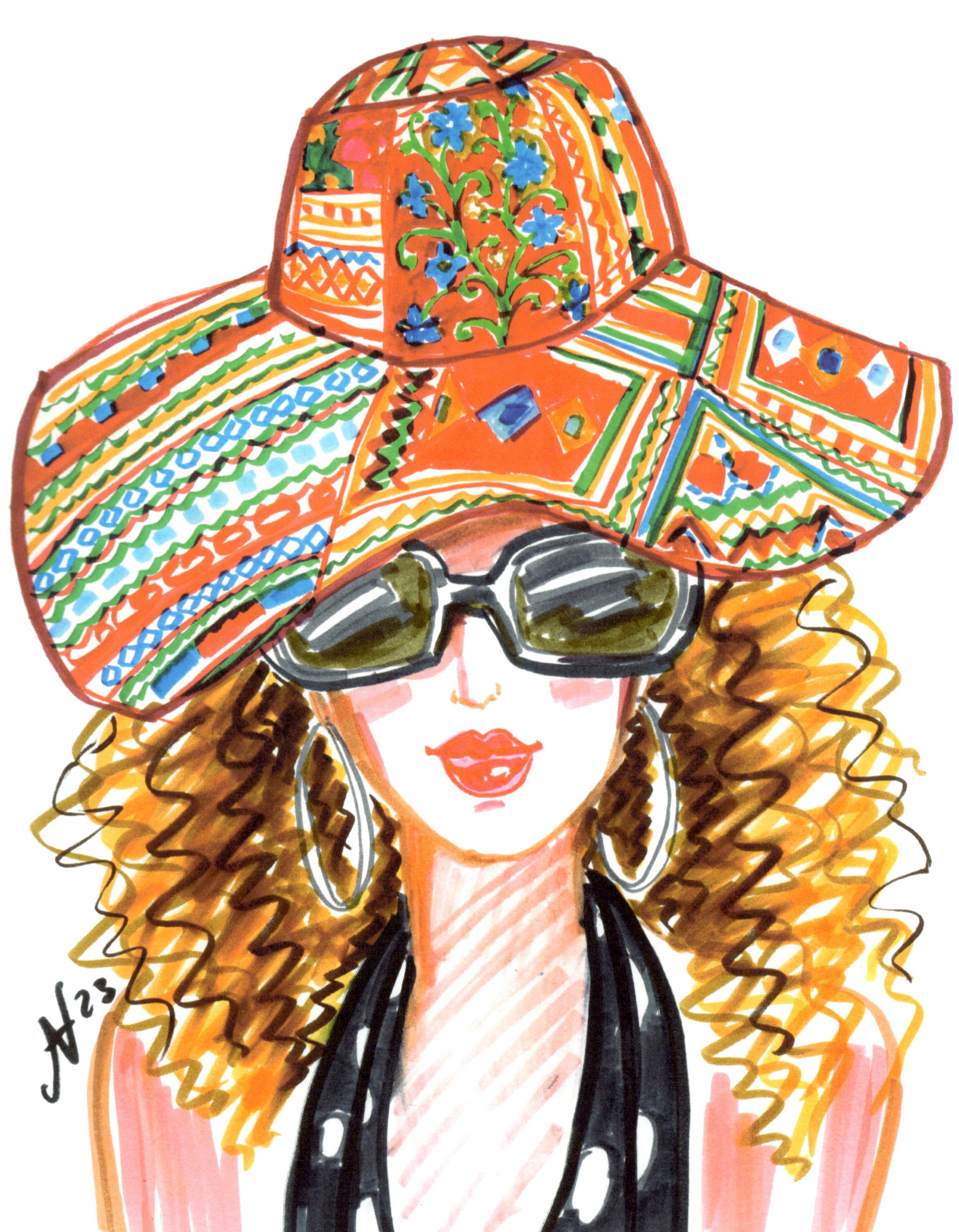

Patchwork Print

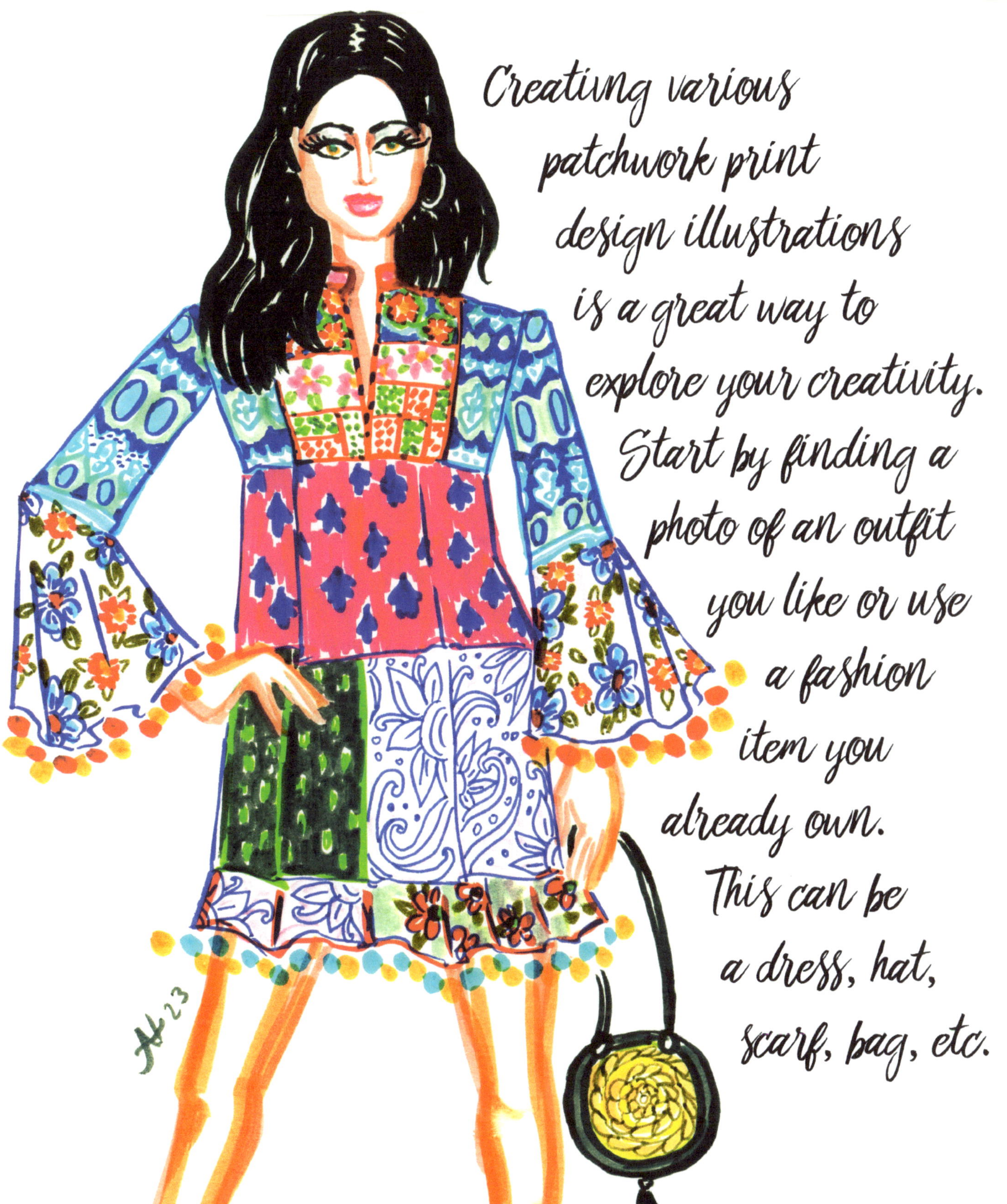

Creating various patchwork print design illustrations is a great way to explore your creativity. Start by finding a photo of an outfit you like or use a fashion item you already own. This can be a dress, hat, scarf, bag, etc.

MENSWEAR

When you draw menswear, make bold, clean lines. Don't give too much detail to the face. No eyelashes, lip color, lip liner, etc. Draw simpler poses, with less expression than female poses. You want to project a masculine image.

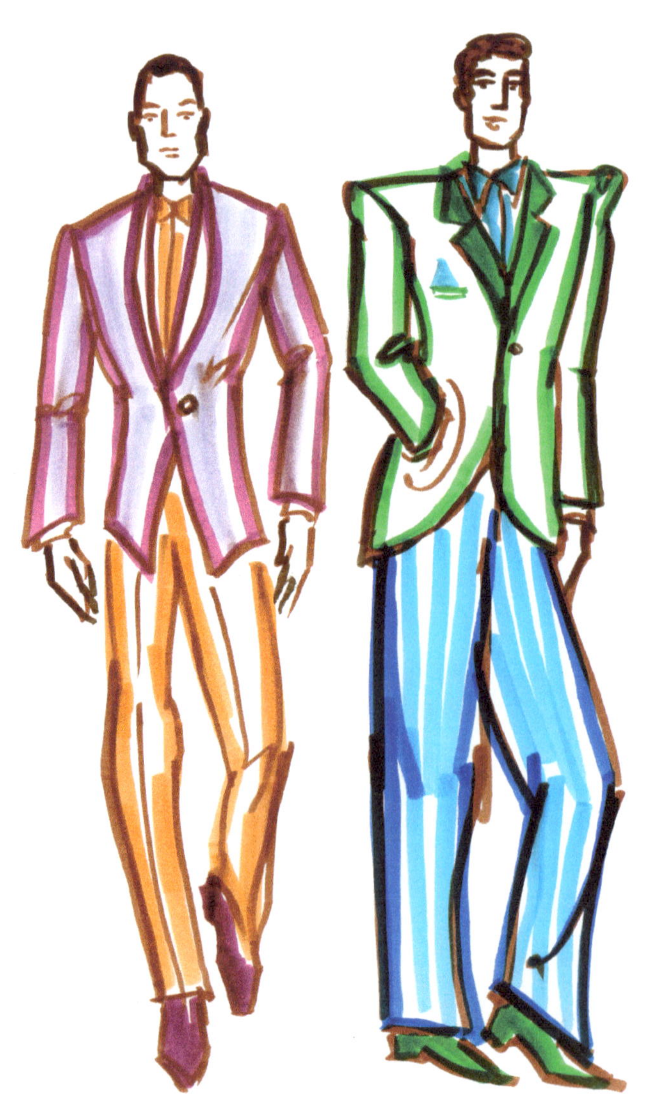

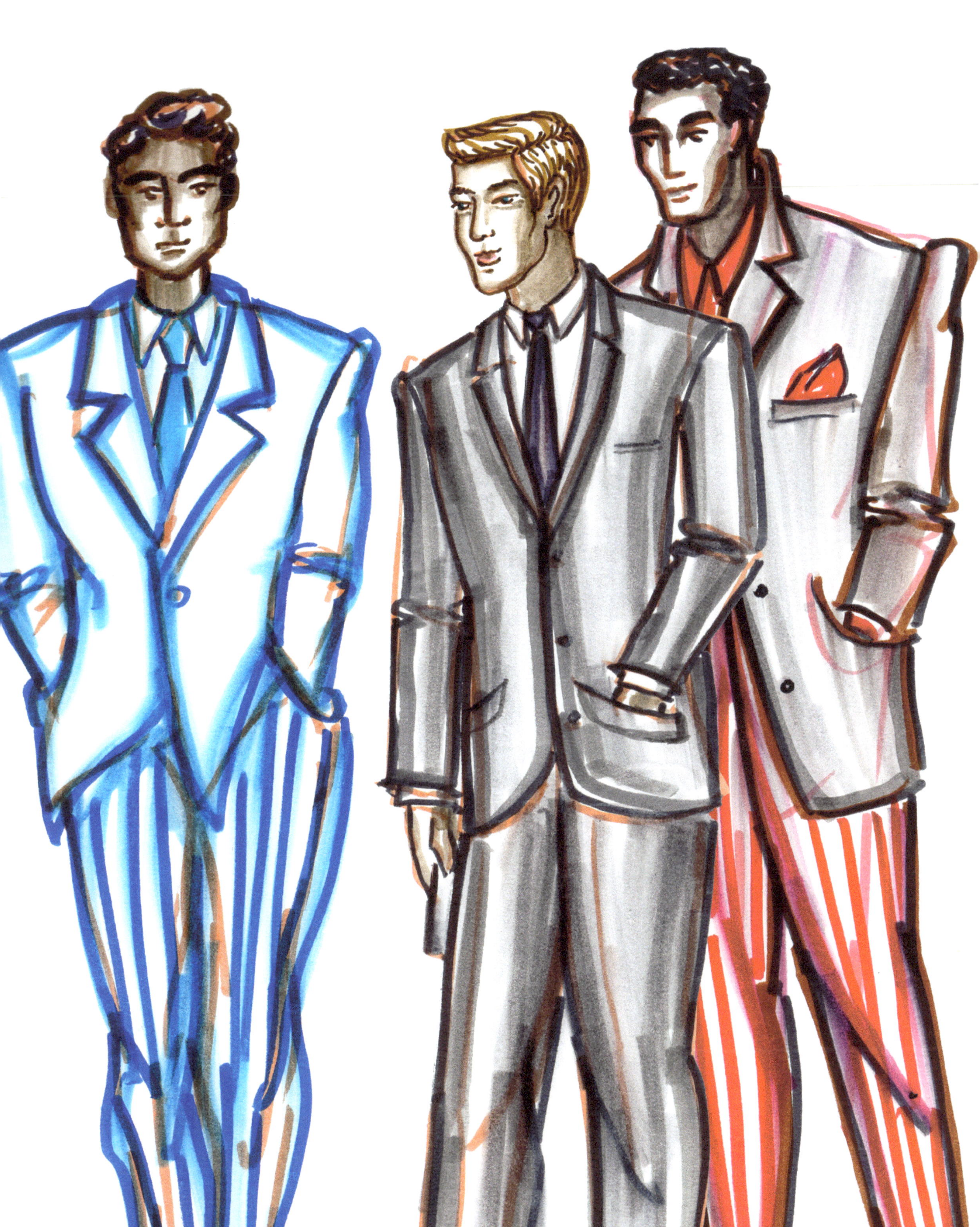

Jewel Tones

When we illustrate fashion and create fashion designs, let's keep in mind the color combinations that look beautiful together. Jewel tones are vibrant shades of blue, green and purple that look wonderful together.

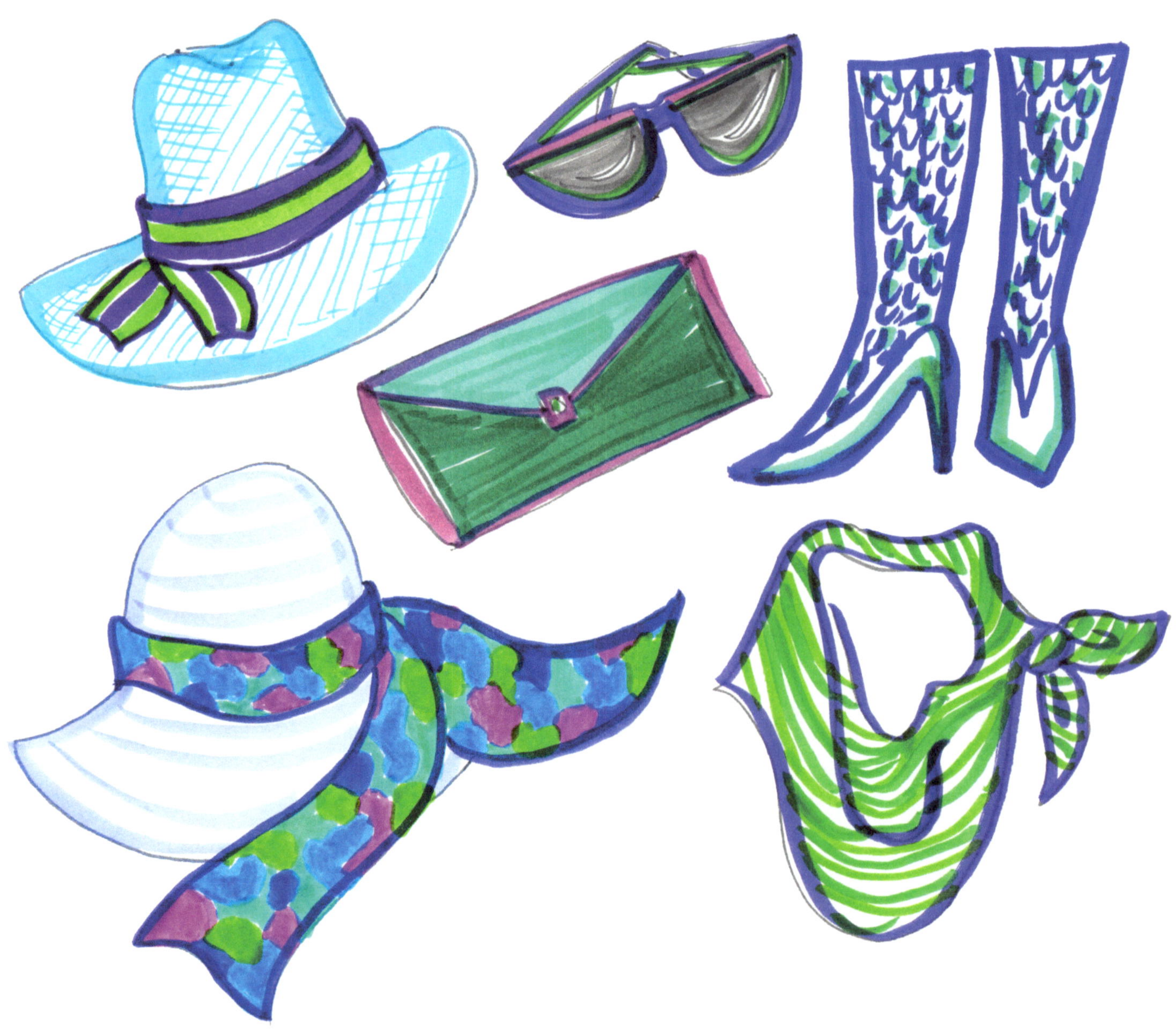

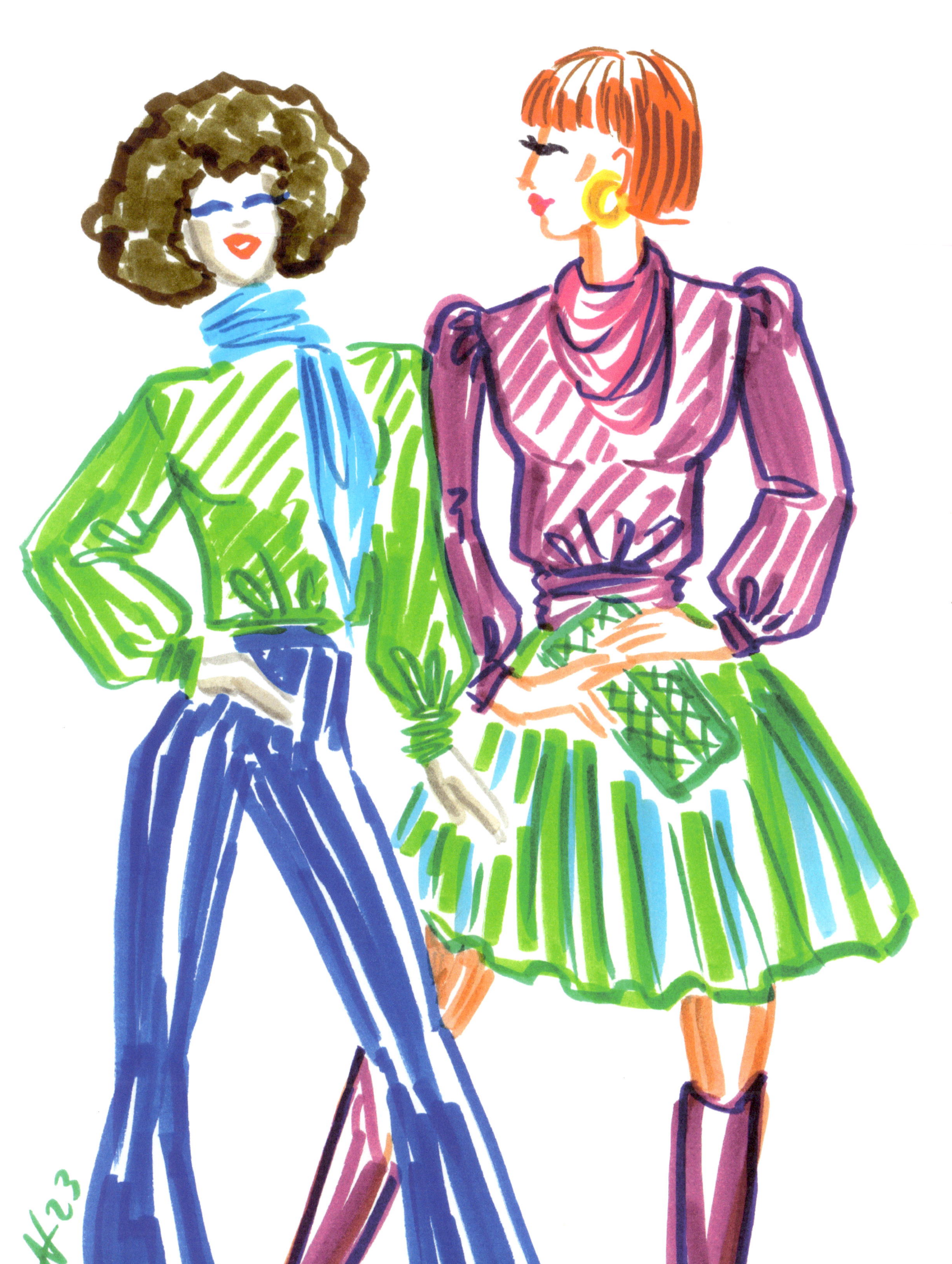

Red & Pink Tones

Reds and pinks, with accents of yellow bring brightness and warmth to fashion illustrations. These colors work great when combined.

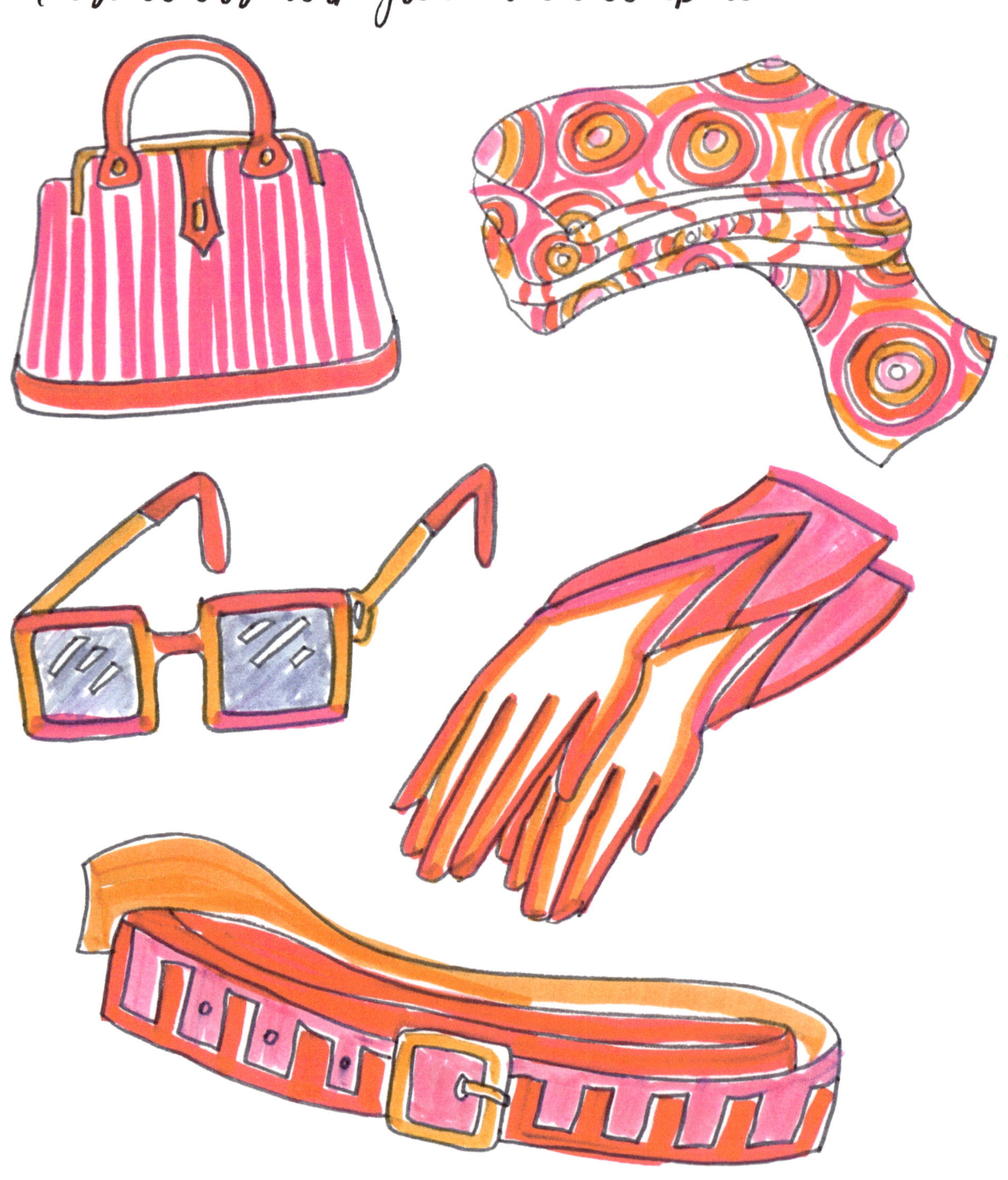

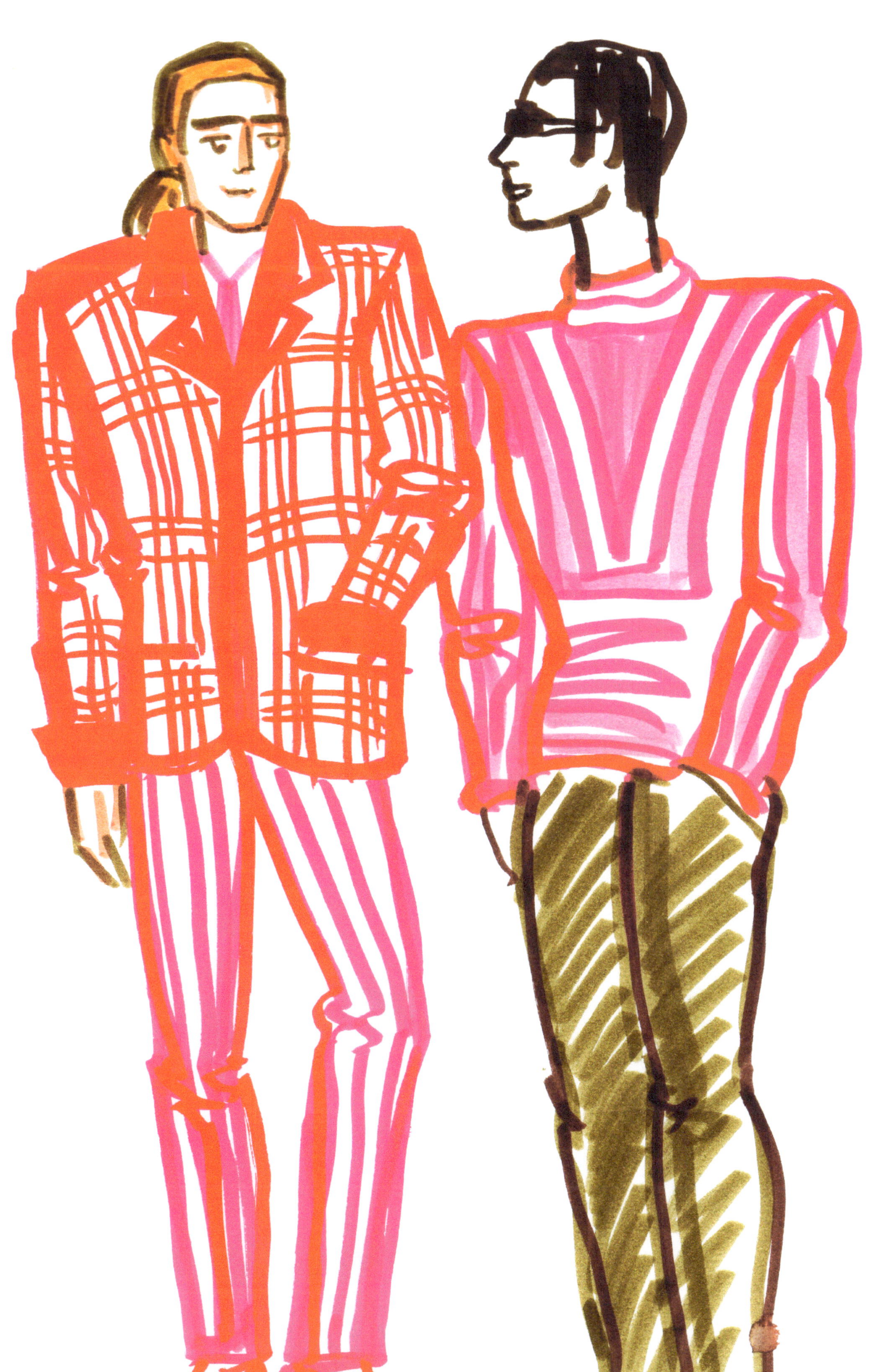

Watercolor Effects

Along with our brush markers, we can use water-filled brush pens to create a watercolor effect by blending water with these markers.

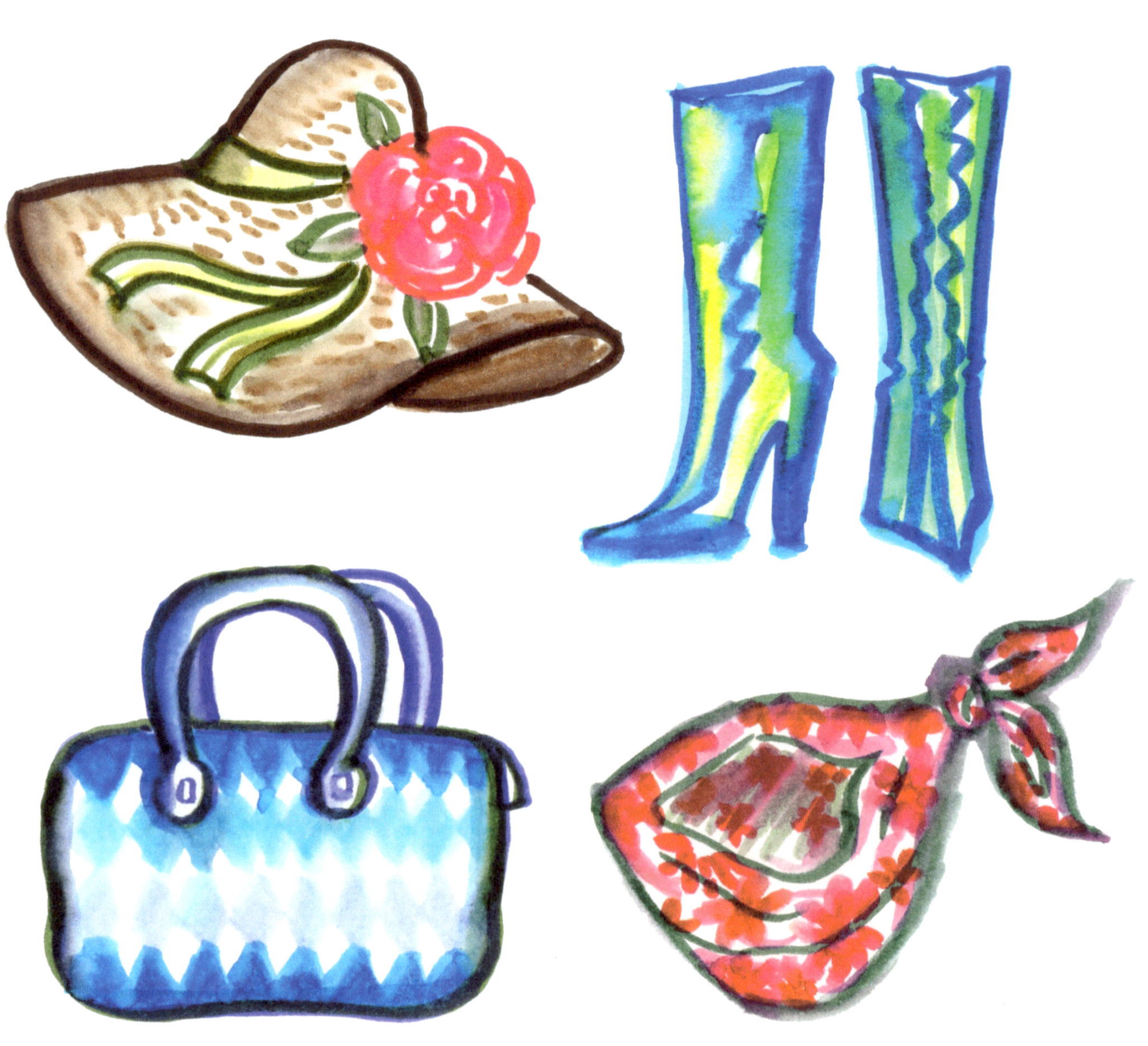

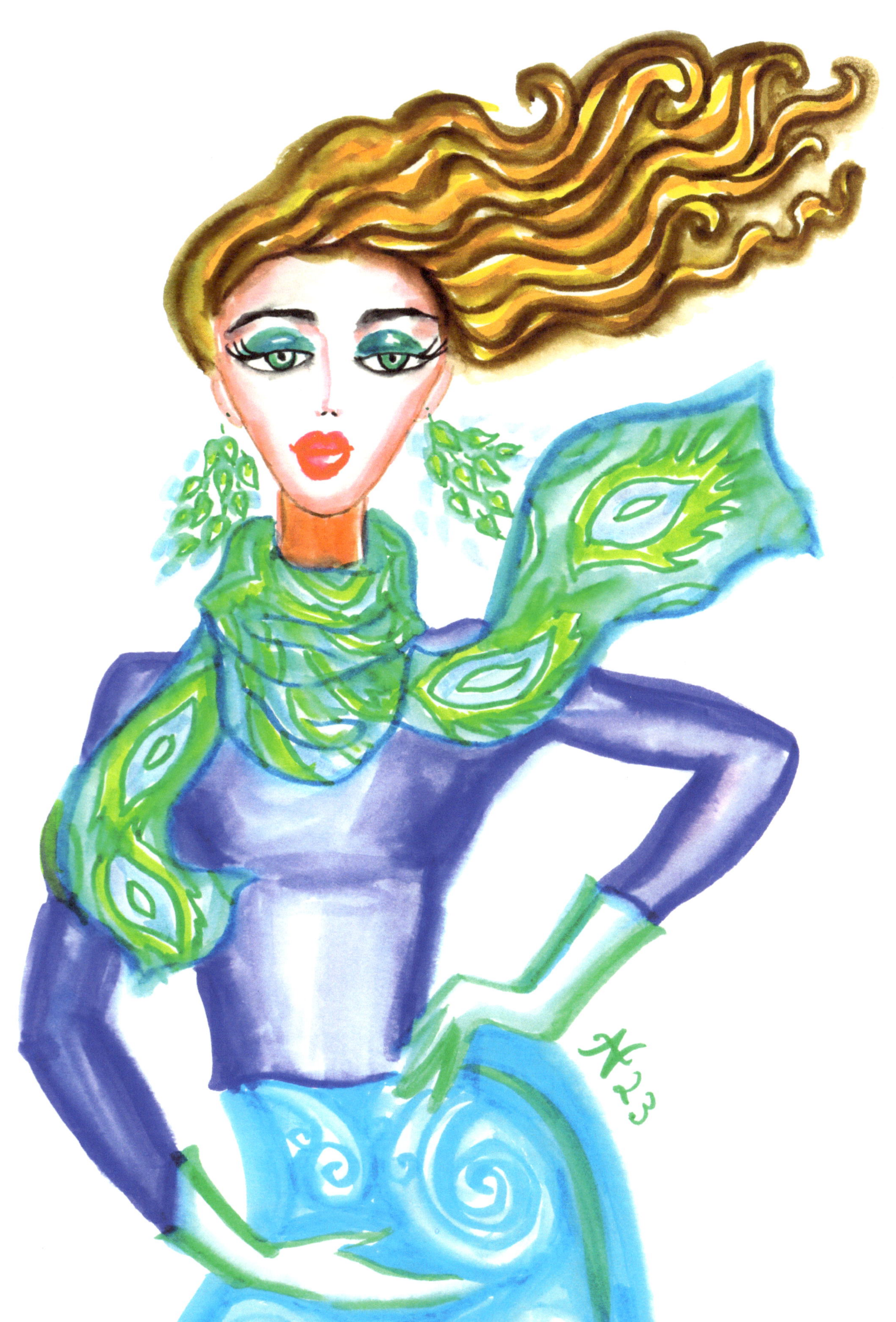

Creative Art Style

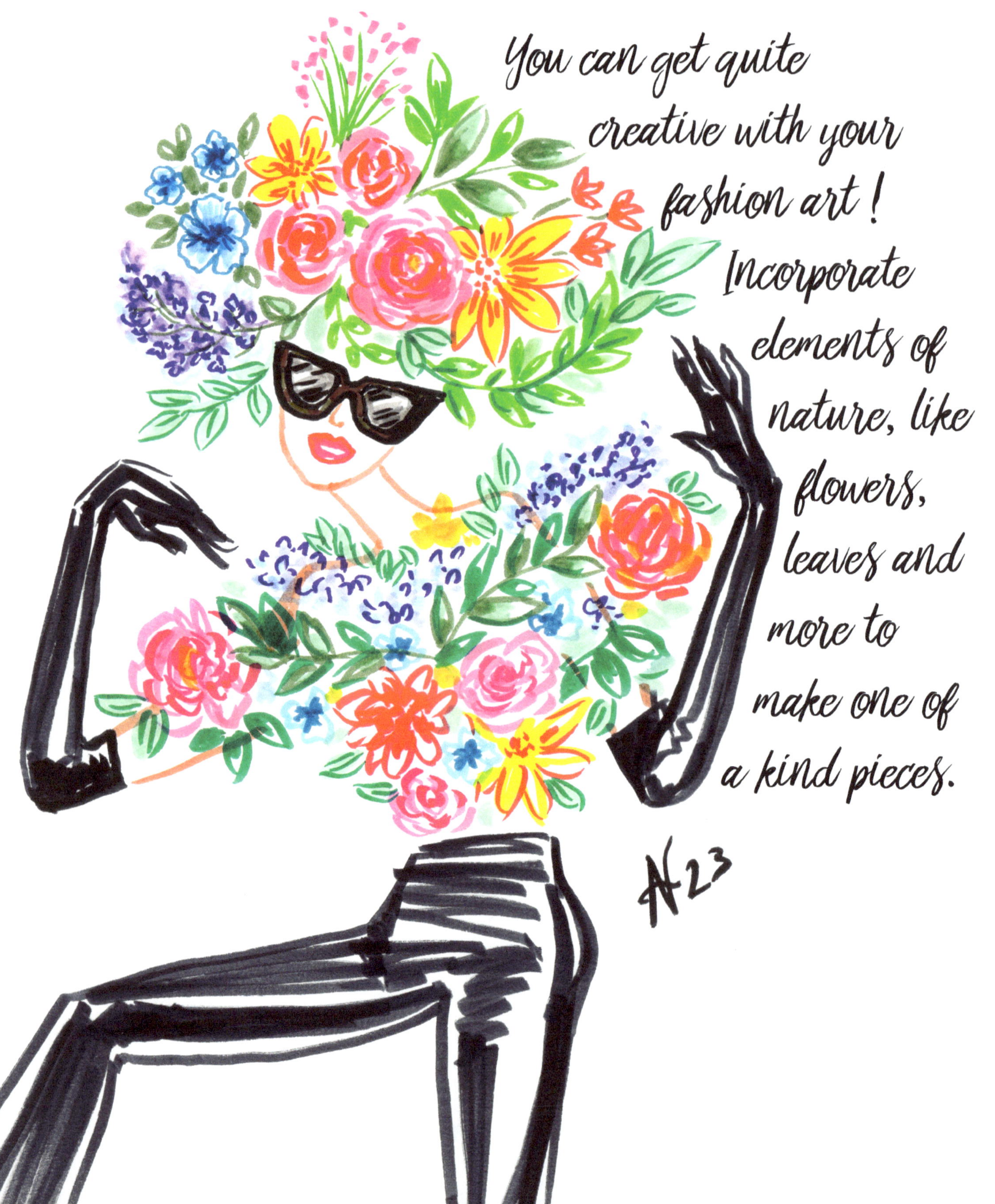

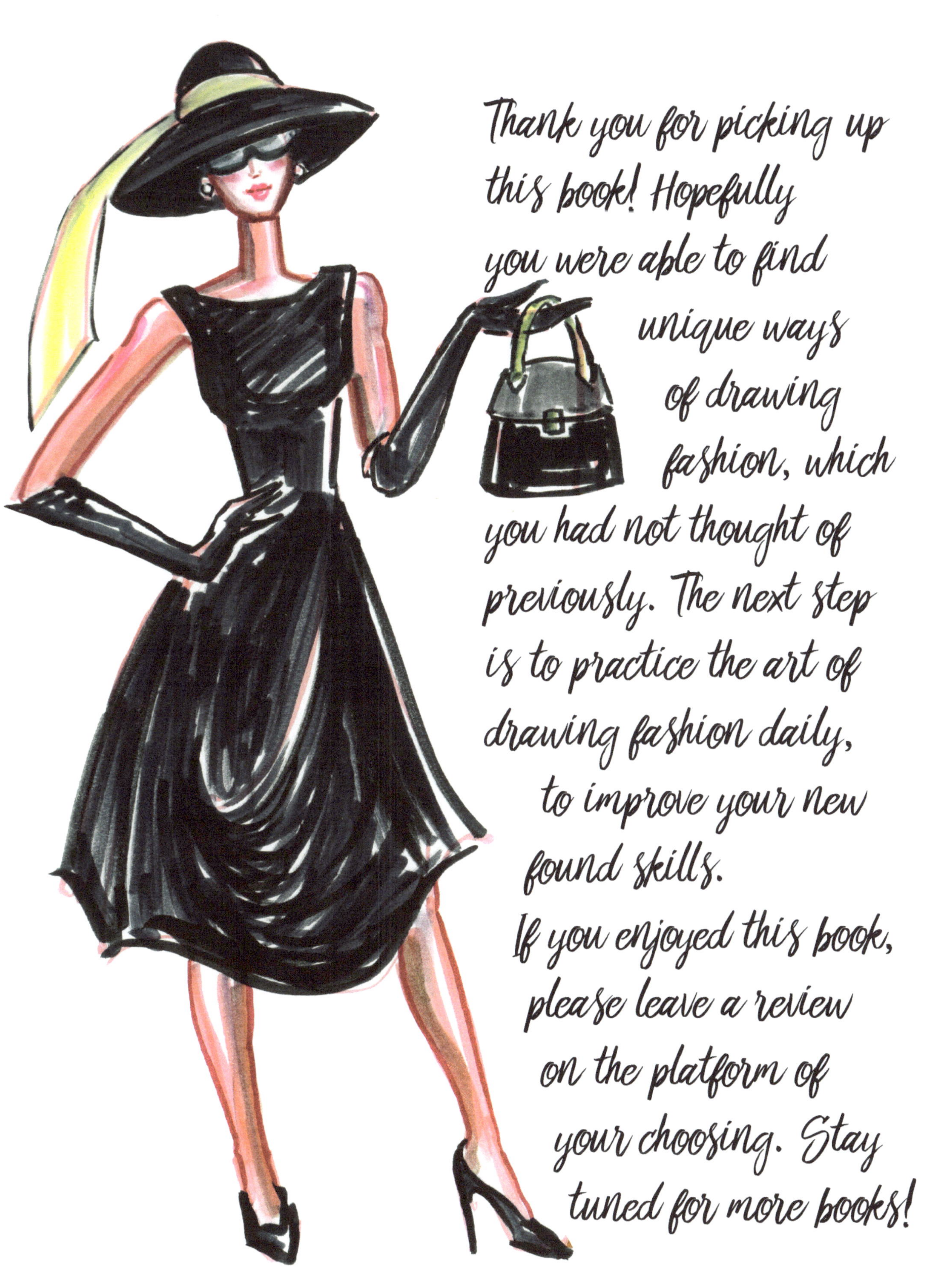
Thank you for picking up
this book! Hopefully
you were able to find
unique ways
of drawing
fashion, which
you had not thought of
previously. The next step
is to practice the art of
drawing fashion daily,
to improve your new
found skills.
If you enjoyed this book,
please leave a review
on the platform of
your choosing. Stay
tuned for more books!

www.ingramcontent.com/pod-product-compliance
Lightning Source LLC
Chambersburg PA
CBHW042127030726
47599CB00002B/378